Academy of Business Research Fall 2015 Conference

October 28-30, 2015

Drury Plaza

San Antonio, TX

Conference Program*

*The conference proceedings will be published and indexed by January 1ˢᵗ on our website and print editions will be available on amazon.com for $5.

Sponsors and Supporters

Academy of Business Research would like to thank
the following companies and organizations
for sponsoring the Fall 2015 Conference:

American Finance Association

Cabells Publishing (www.cabells.com)

Decision Sciences Institute

European Financial Management Association

Financial Management Association

IvyExec.com

Journal of Finance

Silver Wheaton

Social Science Resource Network

Southern Journal of Business and Economics

Wohl Publishing

Conference Staff

Conference Chair
Randall Valentine, Ph.D.

Support Staff
Neelam Kumar Dhungel

Ruth Reich

Dawn Valentine, Ph.D.

Meredith Wilson

We Are Pleased To Announce The Publication Of

Proven student satisfaction. Students actually enjoy reading this book. There is **less frustration** because the problems and questions have been carefully designed to fit the discussion in the text. The result is **a more successful class.**

To learn more about the fourth edition of this outstanding textbook, please visit our website at www.wohlpublishing.com/emery, or email us at instructorsupport@wohlpublishing.com

Conference Social Activities

Registration: 9:00-4:30

Daily Outside Room 62

Wednesday 5:30-6:30 PM

Reception with Bar at Drury 2nd Floor

Thursday 5:30 PM

Awards Reception at Drury 2nd Floor

Followed by Dinner at 7:00 PM

For the Latest Conference Updates Please Subscribe to our Twitter @abr_info

Journal Special Editions

Journal of Marketing Perspectives

The *Journal of Marketing Perspectives* will publish a special edition for papers focusing on case studies in marketing Spring 2016 **Article submissions are due by April 1.**

Journal of Applied Financial Research

The *Journal of Applied Financial Research* will publish a special edition for papers focusing on Currency Risk in Spring 2016. **Article submissions are due December 1.**

Future Conference Dates

Academy of Business Research

Spring 2016 Meeting

New Orleans, LA

March 23-25

www.academyofbusinessresearch.com

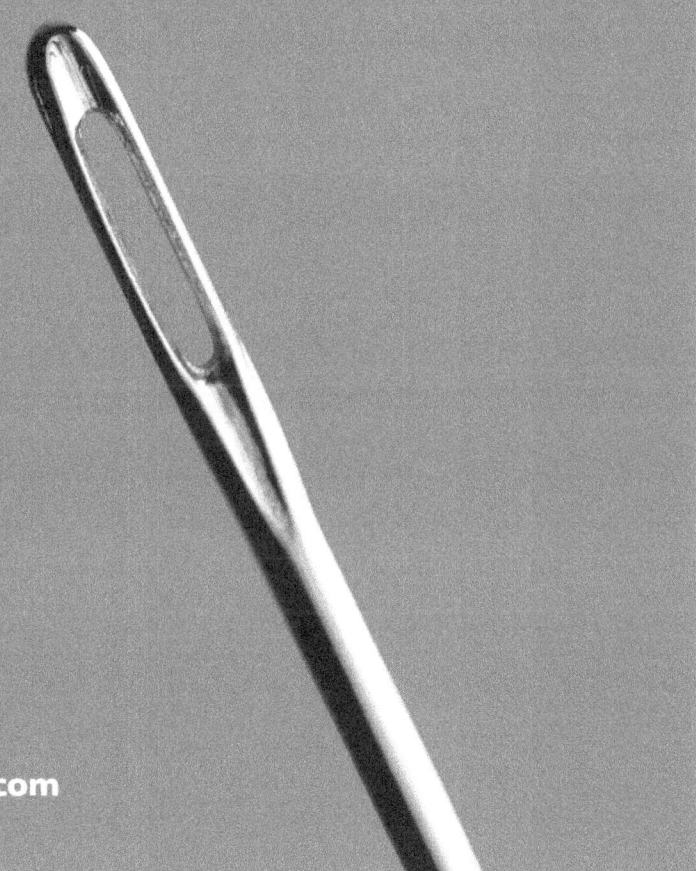

10:00 AM Wednesday October 28th

River Level Room 63

Sponsor: Wohl Publishing

Finance/Real Estate

Session Chair: Tim Wilson, Texas A&M University - Commerce

**Has the Failure to Resolve Conservatorship of Fannie Mae and Freddie Mac
Lead to the De Facto Nationalization of Residential Mortgage Lending**
J. Keith Baker, North Lake College
Pamela Baker, Texas Woman's University

Pay-for-Performance Incentives in the Finance Sector and the Financial Crisis
Satish Thosar, University of Redlands
Sanjiv Jaggia, California Polytechnic State University – San Luis

Capital Exile, Tax Equity, and the 2016 Presidential Election
Tim Wilson, Texas A&M University - Commerce

Covert Examinations: A Balance between Corporate Governance and Privacy
Tim Wilson, Texas A&M University – Commerce

1:00 PM Wednesday October 28th

River Level Room 63

Sponsor: Journal of Marketing Perspectives

Management/Education/Marketing

Session Chair:

Cross-sex Bias in Perceptions of Authentic Leadership
Esther Gergen, Our Lady of the Lake University
Yu Sun, Our Lady of the Lake University
Sandra Tibbs, Our Lady of the Lake University
Mark T. Green, Our Lady of the Lake University

Authentic and Transformational Leadership – An Analysis of the Factor Structures of the Authentic Leadership Questionnaire and Multifactor Leadership Questionnaire
Yu Sun, Our Lady of the Lake University
Esther Gergen, Our Lady of the Lake University
Phyllis Duncan, Our Lady of the Lake University
Meghan Carmody-Bubb, Our Lady of the Lake University
Mark T. Green, Our Lady of the Lake University

The Effects of Cross Cultural Activities on University Students: An Exploratory Study (Skype)
Ina Freeman, Rockford University
Mirela Zimani Papandereou, Rockford University

Does Profit Maximization Determine Sustainability? - An Examination
John H Nugent, Texas Woman's University
Gilbert Werema, Texas Woman's University

A Comparison of Consumer Perceptions of Brand Mention in Magazines between High Involvement and Low Involvement Products
Charles Quigley, Jr., Bryant University
Sharmin Attaran, Bryant University
Elaine Notarantonio, Bryant University

10:00 AM Thursday October 29th

River Level Room 62

Sponsor: Cabell's Publishing

Management/Strategy

Session Chair: S. M. Jameel Hasan, Eastern Washington University

How Do Firms Compete? The Case of China's Emerging Air Purifier Industry
Chuanyin Xie, University of Tampa

Millenials and Occupational Fraud: The Perfect Storm?
Carolyn Conn, St. Edward's University

Building Tacit Knowledge Programs for B-Schools
Phil Lewis, Oklahoma Christian University

How the Media Molds Our Values: The Ethics of Media Manipulation
Ehsan Salek, Virginia Wesleyan College
Kathryn March, Virginia Wesleyan College

What Research Says About: Is Trust Truly Essential to Organizational Functioning or Even to Effective Leadership of the 21st Century Organizations?
S. M. Jameel Hasan, Eastern Washington University
Dean Kiefer, Eastern Washington University

10:00 AM Thursday October 29th

River Level Room 63

Sponsor: Wohl Publishing

Accounting

Session Chair: Paula Diane Parker, University of Southern Mississippi

A Comparison of Professor, Administrator and Student Impressions of the Desirability and Efficacy of the Online Classroom for Accounting Classes
Pamela Baker, Texas Woman's University

An Investigation into the Cause and Remedy to Corporate Inversions
Janet Forney, Truett McConnell College

An Empirical Examination of the Impact of Financial Health on the Explanation of the Discount Rate for Defined Benefit Plans
Paula Diane Parker, University of Southern Mississippi
Nancy J. Swanson, Valdosta State University
Michael T. Dugan, Georgia Regents University

River Level Room 41

Sponsor: Silver Wheaton

Online Business/Marketing

Session Chair: Dawn Valentine, William Carey University

Marketing Mistakes: A Cross Cultural Comparison
Dawn Valentine, William Carey University
Cecilia Maldonado, Georgia Southwestern State University

The Effect of Language in Pop Stars' Social Media
Cecilia Maldonado, Georgia Southwestern State University
Dawn Valentine, William Carey University

A Study of Respondent's Virtual Social Interaction, Leadership Style, and Moral Development
Charles R. Salter, Schreiner University
Mary H. Harris, Cabrini University
Mark Woodhull, Schreiner University
Dan Coleman, Schreiner University

Social Media Rating Sites and Female Consumer Behavior: Marketing Research on Social Media Rating Sites and Its Influence on Female Consumer Behavior and Pre- and Post Purchasing Decisions
D. Anthony Miles, Miles Development Industries Corporation

1:00 PM Thursday October 29th

River Level Room 63

Sponsor: Ivy Exec

Management/Health Care

Session Chair: Rick Richardson, Tarleton State University

Self-Efficacy and Authentic Leadership: Predicting Leader Effectiveness in Dentistry
Jared Montoya, Our Lady of the Lake University
Bernado de la Garza, Our Lady of the Lake University

**Sustainable Business Environment: The Example of La
Defense Planned Business District**
Saba Bahouth, University of Central Oklahoma
Juliette Lloyd, University of Central Oklahoma
Danielle Williams, University of Central Oklahoma

**Decision Making in Commercial Banks: The Role of Adaptive Learning and
Hindsight Bias in Strategic Resource Movement**
John Orr, Webster University
Mark S. Fellhauer, Webster University

**Does Organizational Structure Affect the Relationship between the Investment of
Information Systems and Operational Capability?**
Taeuk Kang, University of Tennessee at Martin
Jonghak Sun, Weber State University
Hui-chuan Chen, University of Tennessee at Martin

The Status of Workplace Bullying in United States State Court Cases
Rick Richardson, Tarleton State University
Reggie Hall, Tarleton State University
Sue Joiner, Tarleton State University

1:00 PM Thursday October 29th

River Level Room 62

Sponsor: Southern Journal of Business and Economics

Accounting

Session Chair:

Taxation in Retirement: What you have to look forward to!!
Carl "Glen" Cooley, Northwestern State University

The Trade-off Between Auditor Conservatism and Audit Accuracy:
Evidence from Going-Concern Audit Errors
Paul Wertheim, Abilene Christian University
Curtis E. Clements, Abilene Christian University
John D. Neill, Abilene Christian University

Director Tenure and Corporate Governance Effectiveness
Paul Wertheim, Abilene Christian University
Curtis E. Clements, Abilene Christian University
John D. Neill, Abilene Christian University

Relevance Regained? The Contents of Introduction to Management Accounting
Michael J. Fischer, St. Bonaventure University

1:00 PM Thursday October 29th
River Level Room 41
Sponsor: Journal of Marketing Perspectives
Marketing

Session Chair: Kevin E. McEvoy, University of Connecticut

How to Get Away with Murder in Marketing? A Framework for Using Forensic Investigation Methods for Examining Marketing Problems
D. Anthony Miles, Miles Development Industries Corporation

Management Incompetence and Employee Distrust? A Baldrige Assessment and Research Study on an Organization in a Management Crisis
Terrell Seaton, Duquesne University
D. Anthony Miles, Miles Development Industries Corporation

Discmania's Instagram Strategy
Scott. D. Roberts, University of the Incarnate Word
Kasey Wolf, University of the Incarnate Word

Pirates of the Couponers: The Curse of the Coupon Black Market
Kevin McEvoy, University of Connecticut

3:00 PM Thursday October 29th
River Level Room 62
Sponsor: Silver Wheaton
Finance

Session Chair: Richard Hurley, University of Connecticut

Examining the Golden Triangle's Historically High Rate of Unemployment
James Slaydon, Lamar University
Carl Montano, Lamar University
Ashraf El-Houbi, Lamar University

Risk Tolerance, Personal Financial Knowledge and Demographic Characteristics- Evidence from India
Sriharsha Reddy, Institute of Management Technology (IMT), Hyderabad
Mousumi Singha Mahapatra, Indian Council of Social Science Research (ICSSR), National Institute of Technology, Durgapur

Consumer Bank Preferences
Jim Bexley, Sam Houston State University
Karen Sherrill, Sam Houston State University

Collusion and Penalties from Foreign Exchange Trades within the Banking Sector
Richard Hurley, University of Connecticut
Pamela Hurley, University Houston - Downtown

3:00 PM Thursday October 29th

River Level Room 63

Sponsor: Academy of Business Research Journal

Education/Management

Session Chair:

Proclivity of Dashboard Usage with ERP
Robert Burdwell, Texas A & M University – San Antonio
Bethuel R. Vinaja, Texas A & M University – San Antonio

Equity Auction Exercise
Jeff Donaldson, University of Tampa
Donald Flagg, University of Tampa

Approaches to Using Comics (Graphic Narratives) in Business Education
Janice L. Ammons, Quinnipiac University
Kurt Shaffert, Yale Divinity School, VAConnecticut Health Care Services

An Analysis of Faith as an Integral Tool of the Socialization of MBA Students
Ivonne A. Delgado-Perez, Concordia University Texas
Charita Ray-Blakely, Concordia University Texas

Profile of the Small Business Entrepreneur:
An Exploratory Study of the Municipalities of Hatillo and Barranquitas, Puerto Rico
Ivonne A. Delgado, Concordia University Texas
Wilfredo Zayas, Inter American University of Puerto Rico

Free to Choose: Factors Driving Student Choice of Online Learning
Adrian Guardia, Texas A & M University – San Antonio
Bethuel R. Vinaja, Texas A & M University – San Antonio
Leonard G. Love, Texas A & M University – San Antonio

6:30 PM Thursday October 29th

Awards Reception Followed by

Dinner at 7:00

9:00 AM Friday October 30th

River Level Room 62

Sponsor: Silver Wheaton

Financial Economics

Session Chair:

U.S. Credit Unions: Size, Growth and Business Strategy
R. Raymond Sant, St. Edward's University
Stephen Bryce Carter, Austin, TX

Determinants of Currency Crises in Mexico: What do we know?
Alicia Rodriguez de Rubio, University of the Incarnate Word

Money Demand in Korea: A Cointergration Analysis, 1973-2014
Miguel Ramirez, Trinity College
Chloe Cho, Trinity College

Grantor Retained Annuity Trusts (GRAT'S) – Are There Really Any Shortcomings?
James D Harriss, Campbell University
Oris L Odom, Cameron University

Transfer Pricing: Oil and Gas vs. Pharmaceuticals
April Poe, University of the Incarnate Word

11:00 AM Friday October 30th

River Level Room 62

Sponsor: Academy of Business Research Journal

Management/Strategy

Session Chair: Leonel Prieto, Texas A& M International University

Contingency Approaches to Structuring New Ventures in Turbulent Environment
Ayishat Omar, Morgan State University
Robert P. Singh, Morgan State University

Managing Self-Efficacy with Transformational Transactional Leadership Effectiveness – An Inspirational Concept
Hamid Khan, Our Lady of the Lake University

The Impact of the Sarbanes Oxley Act on Organizational Structures
Yetunde H. Orimoloye, Morgan State University
Robert P. Singh, Morgan State University

Union and Organizational Commitment as Concurrent Attitudes: A Study of a Midwest Teamsters Local
Bradley M, Thomas, Webster University
John Orr, Webster University
Eric Rhiney, Webster University

Entrepreneurs' Changing Realities: A Parallax View
Leonel Prieto, Texas A& M International University

11:00 AM Friday October 30th

River Level Room 63

Sponsor: Cabell's Publishing

Education/Marketing

Session Chair: Timothy W. Scales, Indiana University East

**Creating a Comprehensive School Support Program to Address
Students' Needs and Increase Retention**
Chin-Yen Alice Liu, Texas A&M University – San Antonio
Leonard G. Love, Texas A&M University – San Antonio
Josephine Sosa-Fey, Texas A&M University – San Antonio

Study Abroad: Higher Education's Differentiator
Warren Matthews, Belhaven University
Jeff Pendo, Education First College Study Tours
Paul Hopkinson, Education First College Study Tours

Student Expectations—Are They Yours?
Barbara Dalby, University of Mary Hardin Baylor
Angela Patrick, Texas A&M University Central Texas

**The Influence of Social Networks on Drip Irrigation Water Conservation
Workshops in the Plano, Texas Area**
Julie Haworth, University of Texas at Dallas

The Reality Store Revised
Tim Scales, Indiana University East

Name	Affiliation	Page
Ammons, Janice L.	Quinnipiac University	18
Attaran, Sharmin	Bryant University	10
Bahouth, Saba	University of Central Oklahoma	14
Baker, J. Keith	North Lake College	9
Baker, Pamela	Texas Woman's University	9, 12
Bexley, Jim	Sam Houston State University	17
Burdwell, Robert	Texas A & M University – San Antonio	18
Carmody-Bubb, Meghan	Our Lady of the Lake University	10
Carter, Stephen Bryce	Austin, TX	20
Chen, Hui-chuan	University of Tennessee at Martin	14
Cho, Chloe	Trinity College	20
Clements, Curtis E.	Abilene Christian University	15
Coleman, Dan	Schreiner University	13
Conn, Carolyn	St. Edward's University	11
Cooley, Carl "Glen"	Northwestern State University	15
Dalby, Barbara	University of Mary Hardin Baylor	22
de la Garza, Bernado	Our Lady of the Lake University	14
Delgado-Perez, Ivonne	Concordia University Texas	18
Donaldson, Jeff	University of Tampa	18
Dugan, Michael T.	University of Southern Mississippi	12
Duncan, Phyllis	Our Lady of the Lake University	10
El-Houbi, Ashraf	Lamar University	17
Fellhauer, Mark S.	Webster University	14
Fischer, Michael J.	St. Bonaventure University	15
Flagg, Donald	University of Tampa	18
Forney, Janet	Truett McConnell College	12
Freeman, Ina	Rockford University	10
Gergen, Ester	Our Lady of the Lake University	10
Green, Mark T.	Our Lady of the Lake University	10
Guardia, Adrian	Texas A & M University – San Antonio	18
Hall, Reggie	Tarleton State University	14
Harris, Mary H.	Cabrini University	13
Harriss, James D.	Campbell University	18
Hasan, S. M. Jameel	Eastern Washington University	11
Haworth, Julie	University of Texas at Dallas	22
Hopkinson, Paul	Education First College Study Tours	22
Hurley, Pamela	University Houston - Downtown	17
Hurley, Richard	University of Connecticut	17
Jaggia, Sanjiv	California Polytechnic State University - San Luis	9
Joiner, Sue	Tarleton State University	14
Kang, Taeuk	University of Tennessee at Martin	14
Khan, Hamid	Our Lady of the Lake University	21
Kiefer, Dean	Eastern Washington University	11

Lewis, Phil	Oklahoma Christian University	11
Liu, Chin-Yen Alice	Texas A&M University – San Antonio	22
Lloyd, Juliette	University of Central Oklahoma	14
Love, Leonard G.	Texas A&M University – San Antonio	18, 22
Mahapatra, Mousumi Singha	Indian Council of Social Science Research (ICSSR), National Institute of Technology, Durgapur	17
Maldonado, Cecilia	William Carey University	13
March, Kathryn	Virginia Wesleyan College	11
Matthews, Warren	Belhaven University	22
McEvoy, Kevin	University of Connecticut	16
Miles, D. Anthony	Miles Development Industries Corporation	13, 16
Montano, Carl	Lamar University	17
Montoya, Jared	Our Lady of the Lake University	14
Neil, John D.	Abilene Christian University	15
Notarantonio, Elaine	Bryant University	10
Nugent, John H.	Texas Woman's University	10
Odom, Oris L.	Cameron University	18
Omar, Ayishat	Morgan State University	21
Orimoloye, Yetude H.	Morgan State University	21
Orr, John	Webster University	14, 21
Papandereou, Mirela Zimani	Rockford University	10
Parker, Paula Diane	University of Southern Mississippi	12
Patrick, Angela	Texas A&M University Central Texas	22
Penedo, Jeff	Education First College Study Tours	22
Poe, April	University of the Incarnate Word	18
Prieto, Leonel	Texas A& M International University	21
Quigley, Jr., Charles	Bryant University	10
Ramirez, Miguel	Trinity College	20
Ray-Blakely, Charita	Concordia University Texas	18
Reddy, Sriharsha	Institute of Management Technology (IMT), Hyderabad	17
Rhiney, Eric	Webster University	21
Richardson, Rick	Tarleton State University	14
Roberts, Scott D.	University of the Incarnate Word	16
Rodriguez de Rubio, Alicia	University of the Incarnate Word	20
Salek, Ehsan	Virginia Wesleyan College	11
Salter, Charles R.	Schreiner University	13
Sant, R. Raymond	St. Edward's University	20
Scales, Tim	University of Indiana East	22
Seaton, Terrell	Duquesne University	16
Shaffert, Kurt	Yale Divinity School, VAConnecticut Health Care Services	18
Sherrill, Karen	Sam Houston State University	17
Singh, Robert P.	Morgan State University	21
Slaydon, James	Lamar University	17
Sosa-Fey, Josephine	Texas A&M University – San Antonio	22

Sun, Jonghak	Weber State University	14
Sun, Yu	Our Lady of the Lake University	10
Swanson, Nancy J.	University of Southern Mississippi	12
Thomas, Bradley M.	Webster University	21
Thosar, Satish	University of Redlands	9
Tibbs, Sandra	Our Lady of the Lake University	10
Valentine, Dawn	William Carey University	13
Vinaja, Bethuel R.	Texas A & M University – San Antonio	18
Werema, Gilbert	Texas Woman's University	10
Wertheim, Paul	Abilene Christian University	15
Williams, Danielle	University of Central Oklahoma	14
Wilson, Tim	Texas A&M University - Commerce	9
Wolf, Kasey	University of the Incarnate Word	16
Woodhull, Mark	Schreiner University	13
Xie, Chuanyin	University of Tampa	11
Zayas, Wilfredo	Inter American University of Puerto Rico	18

Countries Represented at 2015 Academy of Business Research
Fall Conference

Australia
Brazil
Canada
China
Czech Republic
Denmark
Egypt
France
Germany
India
Indonesia
Iran
Italy
Japan
Kuwait
Lebanon
Mexico
Nepal
Netherlands
Pakistan
Philippines
Poland
Portugal
Saudi Arabia
Senegal
South Korea
Sweden
Switzerland
Thailand
Taiwan
Turkey
United Kingdom
United States
Vietnam

2013 Volume II

Academy of Business Research

Journal

Academy of Business Research Journal

Volume IV
2015

The Mission

The *Academy of Business Research Journal* is an interdisciplinary journal dealing with issues in business and education. Any Best Paper award at an Academy of Business Research conference will automatically be placed into the review process for possible acceptance into the *Academy of Business Research Journal*. Direct submissions to the *Academy of Business Research Journal* are reviewed on a continuing basis. Submissions may be made by submitting a copy of your article either in Microsoft Word or PDF format to info@academyofbusinessresearch.com.

The *Academy of Business Research Journal* is intended for parties that are interested in the practical applications of business and industrial research. The intended readership consists of both researchers and practitioners. The emphasis of the journal is on applications, not the statistical methodology used to derive the applications. Thus, any empirical work should be clearly outlined so that a wide spectrum audience can follow the practical applications of the manuscript.

The mission of the *Academy of Business Research Journal* is to support researchers and practitioners in the application of business and industrial development.

Examples of Topics Included in the Journal

- Accounting
- Business Law
- Economics
- Education
- Finance
- Health Care
- Human Resources
- Management
- MIS
- Marketing
- Operations Management
- Public Administration
- Real Estate
- Strategy

Submission of Articles

The Academy of Business Research is published semi-annually. Articles should be submitted via MS Word format to: info@academyofbusinessresearch.com

All articles must follow APA citations. The specifics are listed on our website www.academyofbusinessresearch.com

Editor: James P. Estes, California State University San Bernardino

Assistant Editor: Meredith R. Wilson

Articles Submitted	**259**
Revise and Re-submit	**73**
Acceptances without Revision	**76**
Overall Acceptance	**29%**

~~Call for Papers~~

Academy of Business Research
Spring 2016 International Conference

New Orleans, LA

March 23-25, 2016

Renaissance Hotel, New Orleans

www.aobronline.com

Deadline

Abstract submissions for the Spring 2016 International Conference are due by February 6, 2016. All completed abstracts must be submitted via email to info@academyofbusinessresearch.com or through this online submission form. Abstracts must include all authors, institutional affiliation, and email information. Acceptance decisions will be made no later than February 13, 2016.

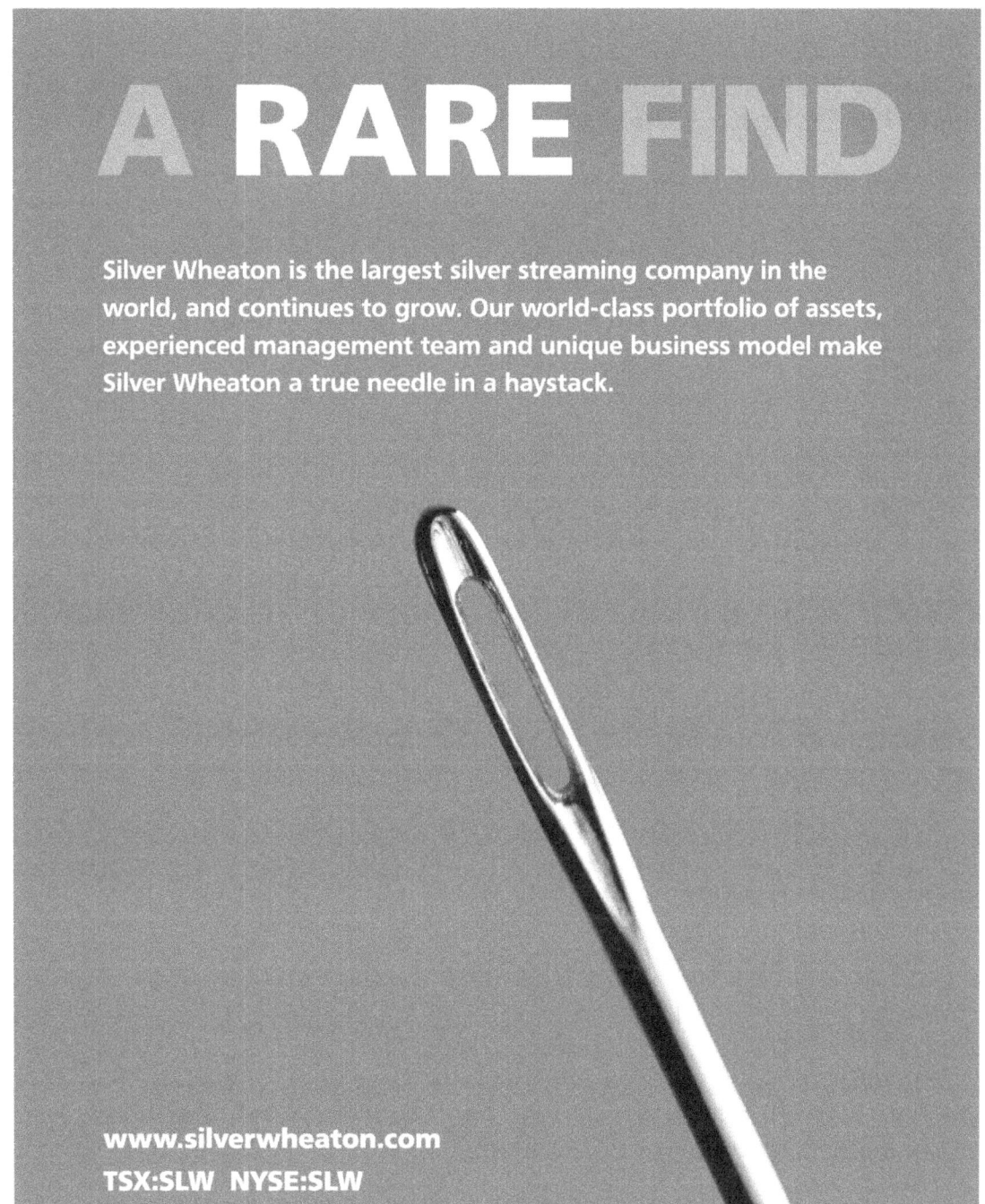

Table of Contents

KIMBERLY DESANTIS, Indiana University East
TIMOTHY W. SCALES, Indiana University East

The Role of Integrity Codes in Times of Changing Technology: Does Anything Make a Difference?

Joann Segovia
Winona State University

Carol Jessup
University of Illinois Springfield

Jim Kroger
Winona State University

ABSTRACT

This article informs accounting professors how to incorporate integrity codes (ethics code, code of conduct) within their classes or for potential admission to a college of business. As AIS professors teach technology, sometimes students become too proficient in its use and could potential unethically use technology to complete assignments or exams. Integrity codes can set a tone within the class or the college of business that will define the expectations of appropriate behavior and potentially resolve potential student integrity violations of using the easily available resources often found on the internet. We discuss the key components of these codes and provide several examples. Finally, anecdotal evidence appears to support the use of integrity codes.

Introduction

"Cheating among students appears widespread and increasing. In some studies, up to 80% of high-achieving high school students and 75% of college students admit to cheating, a percentage that has been rising in the past 50 years (Ohio State, 2009). Another survey reported 75 to 98 percent of college students cheated which is up from only 20% in 1940 (Education Portal, 2011). At times, students search the web to find solutions to homework or quizzes and can successfully find sites to assist them. What constitutes ethical behavior and use of this information? How can code of ethics provide guidance or define the "tone" for the class?

Good Morning America emphasized in the media the prevalence of cheating in colleges and universities with the University of Central Florida example that occurred in the fall 2010 semester (Zaragoza, 2010). This cheating scandal shocked viewers because of the sheer magnitude of students involved, over 600 students in a strategic management course who cheated on the test by shared resources originating from access to the test bank (Postal, 2010). Also, academics and others will find interesting the criticism about the 20-year veteran teacher's use of test banks. The criticism in various forums ranged from making him appear inept and incompetent for using test banks to expressed sympathy for teaching a class of that size.

A follow-up discussion exists as to what constitutes acceptable resources for student study. Colleagues disagree about students finding and using test banks and solution manuals on the internet or elsewhere. Is student resourcefulness wrong? Some thought this behavior was wrong if students paid for the resources; others thought the internet searches were fair study and the mark of a good student to use all available resources. One rare student communicated the following:

> I hate to be the bearer of bad news here but I think there may be an ethical
> issue with the online quiz. I found something on the internet that jeopardizes
> the integrity of the quiz. It would be best if I could explain this to you on
> the phone or in person. Is it possible to call you or you call me?

While taking an online quiz, this student had uncovered a published test bank at a website through a Google search using terms from one question. Upon the professor's contact, the student sent the URL to the website. The professor thanked the student profusely for having integrity and followed up by contacting the second and third author of this popular textbook. The third author's reply indicated that this newly released edition of the textbook and its test bank did not represent a compromised situation. Furthermore, he expanded his response to include that most of these types of problems originated from professors who put materials out on the web and forget about them, enabling the search engines to find the problems and answers. However, this was not the case for this particular URL as the materials for nine chapters of this popular text remained available at the URL at no charge to anyone who found them for several more years. They have since been removed, only because the internet provider merged with another company, disabling the links. The test bank questions for the newest edition are currently available, at other websites.

What might one conclude from this situation? That the student who reported this to his professor exhibited a rare integrity as no statement on the syllabus requested that students report available internet resources. In addition, the textbook authors exhibited a degree of reckless absence of concern about the matter. How can professors use these resources to test students if the internet provides such easy access and the professors feels that the student use results in inappropriate behavior and a potential violation of student integrity?

Potential Steps to Minimize Potential Integrity Violations

A simple Google search of the Internet by the professor will inform the professor whether other professors post solutions on unprotected websites, or some websites offer opportunities to purchase solutions and test banks for the text used within the course. If these resources readily exist on the Internet, professors can create assignments by combining problems within their texts and other texts, but change the name of the company or other unique identifying information so searching for solutions on the Internet becomes more challenging. Also, professors can avoid take-home tests for which students can download answers or essays from an online source. Professors should notify textbook publishing companies of inappropriate websites. Publishers will request the site's author to remove information or will prosecute illegal sale of copyright materials.

The professor could consider establishing an ethical tone within the course. The Sarbanes-Oxley Act that Congress passed in 2002 supports establishment of code of ethics and whistleblowing programs. All U.S. public company boards and their managements must disclose whether or not they have adopted a code of ethics (Section 406) and offer legal protection to whistleblowers who provide evidence of fraud (Section 806). To prepare students for these corporate requirements and to establish the tone of the course, a professor can incorporate these requirements in the course.

The Internet provides many examples of various business schools' codes of conduct. Key components include (1) explicit statements of standards of academic integrity, (2) definitions and examples of cheating, plagiarism, collusion, and other breaches in academic integrity, (3) requirements for students to clarify and inquire possible interpretation for actions, (4) outcomes for infractions, such as expulsion, suspension, or other sanctions, (5) responsibilities and procedures for faculty and students to report infractions or address potential violations, and (6) references to the institutions' posted codes of academic conduct. The college and/or professor can require signed statements recognizing the code of ethics for the admission to the college and/or individual assignments (Segovia, 2010). The feedback from professors at the 2010 Accounting Information Systems Educators Conference who implemented codes of ethics indicate fewer violations and increased understanding by students for the consequences of inappropriate action.

Appendix A provides four examples of integrity codes. The first example represents an example of an integrity code used for admission to the college of business and includes a statement that students must sign to acknowledge that he/she has read the code. The second example represents a college's Business Code of Professionalism. The third example reflects a statement that an accounting professor requires his students to sign at the beginning of the course. An instructor can use the fourth example for individual assignments. Depending upon the institution, students may sign the code for admission into the college and/or for each assignment to remind the student of the expectations.

The ListServe Accounting Education Using Computers and Multimedia (AECM) contains prolific dialogue on all matters related to technology in accounting education. In a search of its archives using the term "cheat", many discussions surface as members readily contribute their various perspectives. Honor codes, webcams to catch cheaters, cell phone use (to allow or not) have all been included in discussion of issues around cheating and plagiarism in the last couple months (AECM 2011). The acceptance of surveillance means such as webcams by honest students was recently discussed, in terms of the honest student's self-interest. Whether high tech or low tech surveillance means are used, the topic of whistleblowing provisions comes to mind.

Whistleblower provisions as used in organization have certain elements considered beneficial to include in the development of such policy. Modeled after corporate policies, elements include provisions to emphasize who is covered, non-retaliation policies, confidentiality, description of the process to be followed, and the communication to stakeholders of its importance (Eaton and Akers, 2007). As with any organization, first create a culture where individuals consider whistleblowing the acceptable norm. If a professor undertakes a whistleblowing policy, one needs to be very careful to determine in advance what constitutes consistent handling of complaints and what will happen if students make false or malicious reports. As one adopts the best practices of public and private organizational policy in place after Sarbanes Oxley, determine the applicability to an academic setting as well the compatibility with a university's existing policies. Parties can misuse any noble policy; thus, investigate the benefits and misuses of whistleblowing in this context.

Examples of Cheating Incidents

The following section provides examples of potential integrity violations within several different accounting courses. In addition, we discuss the resolution of the situation.

The first incident involved two graduate assistants in a ten-week governmental and nonprofit accounting course. Because of the short duration of the course, the professor decided to allow a portion of the final as a take-home exam and included the following statement within this part of the exam: "You are absolutely not to consult any other person about answers to any part of this exam, and you are on your honor to abide by this. Variances will be considered as cheating and will be dealt with accordingly." While grading the test, the professor noted that two students' answers to an opinion-type question on single audits used the same unusual wording. Upon closer verification and examination, the professor found a number of other questions on the two papers contained the same wording and style. The students' actions shocked the professor as both students had excelled in previous coursework and were graduate assistants.

The professor asked the one student (a more easy-going, balanced nature individual) if she wanted to explain anything about the test, as the professor held the student's copy of the test. The student stated emphatically that she had done her own work. When shown the similarity of the wording of the other paper (no name was given), she looked puzzled and admitted that after she completed the exam that she had talked about the test to the other student (who she named), but that she had assumed that the other student was finished. She then further volunteered that she knew that they were not supposed to talk about the exam, and that she should receive a penalty, the same as the other student. When shown that the style of wording was so identical which indicated more than just two people talking generically about the questions, she began to shake with anger, and subsequently to cry. She theorized that since they both worked in the accounting department side by side with their laptops, perhaps the other student had looked at her unattended computer.

The professor confronted the other student (a more compulsive, straight-A driven individual) with the situation two days later. The student stated that she had noticed the other graduate assistant was no longer friendly to her, and would not reply to text messages. Therefore, she knew that suspected cheating was likely an issue, and kept repeating, "You know that I do good work and have done good work in my previous classes with you". When told that was not the issue under deliberation, she shared that she was scared and overwhelmed because of the knowledge of the suicide of a close friend from high school: "I was too upset. I didn't trust my judgment at the time". When asked why she had not instead asked for an extension, she broke down, looked at the professor in horror, stating that she now probably could not get an A. When told instead, that she might be failed for the course, she looked even more distressed. After thinking about the situation for several days, the professor docked the student's course grade a full letter grade.

This is not the end of the story. More information emerged involving another student in the same course when discussing her course grade by email. The third student (a stellar, cheerful, hardworking student who had a difficult pregnancy during the semester) earned a B in the course and was fine with this, given the circumstances. She was requesting a potential job reference for a forthcoming position. In response to the professor's email that commended her continued positive attitude while facing difficult circumstances, she replied to the professor's mention about delaying the release of grades because of suspected cheating in the class with the following remarks:

> That is terrible people would cheat!! There were a few people that asked what I got but I never replied to emails, face book messages, etc. Pointless to give answers to someone that I work hard to get the answers myself! Most of the questions were opinion too, just took time to answer which shouldn't have been an issue! Thank you for letting me know my grades though.

All three students were female, approximately the same age, and among the "best of the best". This highlights that the cheating incident was likely not limited to the two excellent students caught sharing answers but probably was much more pervasive. The third student's comments clearly demonstrate the role that technology plays in the current academic environment and how students use technology and social networking to communicate.

While these incidents can cause professors to feel discouraged about academic integrity violations, one can try to enforce a stronger ethical tone. In the following semester, this professor determined a need for more extensive use of signatures and signed statements for each assignment to highlight the seriousness of any cheating behavior on any work that isn't done face to face. This is in lieu of prior semesters where potential cheating behavior and its consequences is discussed the first day of class and the inclusion of a statement within the course syllabus.

A second example involved a data flow diagram, an end of a chapter exercise from the text. Each student submits a draft of a flowchart for 25% of the grade and then forms a group of 3-4 students to review the individual submissions and arrive at a consensus as to how to best depict the process. The group submission comprises the remaining 75% of the grade.

One resourceful student appeared to search the internet and found the solution posted within a Word document. The assignment required the students to use Excel, a readily available tool used by accountants. The student cut and pasted the "Word" solution to Excel that displayed the results in one cell (see Appendix B). Not only did the student deny pasting the solution in Excel, but insisted that the obvious similarity in descriptions and flow of activities resulted from his MIS major and his excellent understanding of the documentation process. Furthermore, he insisted that this was a case of "he said/she said" and that the professor would never believe he did the work. The latter assessment by the student was correct.

The difficulty of handling the situation compounded as the student provided this "copied" solution to other group members who claimed that they had no knowledge that the first student had found the solution on the Internet. The professor met with the Dean and he also concurred that this obviously was copied work and not the student's work. The student who found the solution and submitted the data flow diagram as his own received a zero for the project. Interestingly, the situation appeared to become known by other students and created an uncomfortable "tone" for the class. The professor also wonders if weak teaching evaluations resulted as the student who appeared to copy the solution was rather outgoing and vocal and perhaps told a different side of the story to fellow class mates.

A third example involved a cheating incident on one of ten 4-point quizzes in an undergraduate accounting information systems course. The course consisted of 420 points, which comprised two 100-point exams, 115 points dispersed between computer assignments (Access, Excel, accounting software), other written assignments, and the quizzes which included dropping the lowest score. The quiz instructions contained the following statement: "You can use your book, notes, but not another person. You also are not to discuss this quiz with anyone else until the quiz has officially ended." In addition, the syllabus contained the business school's code of professionalism which the instructor had discussed. The professor received an email that contained the following:

> I was wondering if you could reset my quiz. I had it open about to start it and I walked away, my cousin took it for me while I walked away trying to be nice. She is a super nerd and also an accounting major. I'm sure she got a lot of them right, but I would like to see the questions and take it myself. Is this possible at all, because I would like to see the questions to study off of. Also, I understand that sending this could result in a zero.

In this case, how should the professor handle the situation? On the one hand, the student has been honest to express the dilemma, but on the other hand, the student shows a blatant disregard for the assessment process as well as presumably the upperclassmen in the same major. This situation was handled with the following response.

> You have voluntarily come forward to let me know about this, posing a situation that makes me conclude that you do know this was not acceptable. I really don't know what the right thing to do is, so it is a dilemma for me. I have decided that I want your work (you are my student, hopefully she is not one of my current or past students - I don't even want to know if she is or was because I would be very saddened by the behavior described). It makes a mockery of what we value in academia, first and foremost which is academic integrity. I am going to recognize the integrity you exhibited in voluntarily acknowledging this, and I will reopen the quiz and decide later if I will let you keep the score that you earn. I imagine there are lessons we are all learning from this, and hope that we can move ahead from this. To give your cousin any benefit of the doubt I would like to think maybe she thought quizzes could be taken repeated times, but in any event, her behavior crossed a line of respecting your boundaries. You appear to have tried to set some limits here with her, and to be as accountable as I guess anyone could

be in this situation, and so again, I commend you for rising to the challenge here. The quiz will be reset, thanks again for your honesty, and simply do your best on the quiz. I will be honest with you - this has very much "rattled" me. As I re-read what I have written here, I believe I have decided that the score you earn will be kept, in an attempt to put this situation behind us, and move ahead. I want you to learn in my course and I want you to learn from every experience you have. I guess we both have learned something this evening. Have a good night.

The student responded that she had learned from the experience, appreciated the professor's email, and expressed again that she was sorry. This situation indicates the precarious balance that professors and students have to navigate to resolve such situations. This demonstrates how unlikely that when faced with these situations that the students and professors can agree whether a situation: 1.) constitutes cheating, and 2.) how the professor should appropriately handle the situation. Certainly, the detection, prevention, and resolution of academic misconduct requires time and energy as well as a creating stressful situations that questions one's decisions and own values.

Does A Code Make A Difference?

The inclusion of a reference to a code of conduct (Appendix A, example #3) has been included on one professor's syllabus for many years. On the first day of class, the professor extensively discusses what the code of conduct means and the expectations for academic conduct for the course, for each major deliverable (homework, projects, or tests). In addition, any electronic work completed for the course includes the following statement highlighted in bold before a student can proceed to any given deliverable:

Finally you are to proceed according to the business school code of professional integrity as outlined in the syllabus. Your clicking on the above link to proceed indicates your understanding and acceptance of the following statement. The attached test is my work. I completed it by myself, without consulting other students, (or their work), faculty or any other person. I also did not share my work with others. I understand that I am free to consult only the following materials: the text for this course, notes from class or the Blackboard, and Blackboard links to materials for this course.

Does use of a repeated statement such as this make a difference? Certainly, this creates a better sense of accountability if a professor catches a student acting inappropriately and deters excuses about allowable or inappropriate behavior. However, even with such statements and precautions, deviations from acceptable conduct will continue to occur. For example, the professor notices that two half-brothers in the course both happen to take the online test at the same time or the awareness that a female student and her boyfriend that sits next to her in class take the online test at the same time. Tools behind the scenes of course management systems verify where people accessed the system; however, at some point, this kind of surveillance becomes very tedious. For example, is it fair to only investigate the two brothers that you know are related? Does increased scrutiny for a few, but not all students constitute inequitable behavior on the part of the professor? For that reason, professors need to include various assessment methods in which students will less likely cheat to ensure that students receive a grade befitting of their own work.

If one integrates a code of conduct or behavior, one needs to avoid too many rules as potential cheaters will look for every loophole that they can find. On the other hand, if one uses a principles based approach to a code, the question as to whether a circumstance constitutes cheating or not surfaces which reflects some of the same issues surrounding principles versus rules based accounting standards.

Conclusion

In conclusion, teaching in the current environment necessitates that accounting professors give sufficient thought and attention as to whether their past methods of ensuring a level playing field for all students are still effective. New technologies, changing student attitudes, and an increased diversity of international students from cultures with varied norms of what constitutes cheating all contribute to the benefit of increased attention to codes of conduct, and their methods of implementation.

References

AECM. (ongoing since 1994). Accounting Education Using Computers and Multimedia. This Listserv is hosted by Loyola College in Maryland. Available from: http://pacioli.loyola.edu/aecm/ December 23, 2014.

Eaton, T. V and Akers, M. D. (June 2007). Whistleblowing and Good Governance: Policies for Universities, Government Entities, and Nonprofit Organizations. *The CPA Journal Online* Available from http://www.nysscpa.org/cpajournal/2007/607/essentials/p58.htm December 23, 2014.

Education Portal. (2011, June 29). 75 to 98 Percent of College Students Have Cheated. Available from http://education-portal.com/articles/75_to_98_Percent_of_College_Students_Have_Cheated.html December 23, 2014.

Ohio State University. (2009, August 12). Epidemic of student cheating can be cured with changes in classroom goals. *ScienceDaily*. Available from http://www.sciencedaily.com/releases/2009/08/090810025249.htm December 23, 2014.

Postal, L. (November 21, 2010). 'Test banks' are at the center of UCF's cheating scandal, *Orlando Sentinel*. Available from: http://articles.orlandosentinel.com/2010-11-21/news/os-ucf-cheating-online-20101121_1_studies-cheating-large-lecture-classes-test-banks December 23, 2014.

Segovia, J. (2010). Technology: Friend or Foe, *Business Education Forum*.

Southern Illinois University Edwardsville (SIUE). (2011). Web page for School of Business, Current Students, Policies and Practices, Code of Professionalism Available from: http://www.siue.edu/business/current/policies_forms.shtml#code December 23, 2014.

Zaragoza, L. (November 8, 2010). UCF probes cheating scandal involving hundreds, *Orlando Sentinel*. Available from: http://articles.orlandosentinel.com/2010-11-08/news/os-ucf-cheating-test-20101108_1_apparent-cheating-exam-students December 23, 2014.

Appendix A: Four Examples of Codes of Ethics
#1 Admission to College of Business:
Academic Honesty

The University expects all students to represent themselves in an honest fashion. In academic work, students are expected to present original ideas and give credit for the ideas of others. The value of a college degree depends on the integrity of the work completed by the student. When an instructor has convincing evidence of cheating or plagiarism, the following actions may be taken: assign a failing grade to the assignment in question, or assign a failing grade for the course in which the student cheated. For informational purposes, instructors may choose to report the offense, the evidence, and their action to the Dean of their college, or the Vice President for Academic Affairs. If the instructor (or any other person) feels the seriousness of the offense warrants a different or additional penalty, the incident may be reported to the Student Conduct Committee through the Student Support Services Office. The Student Conduct Committee will follow procedures set out in the Student Conduct Code. After its review of the case, and a fair and unbiased hearing, the Student Conduct Committee may take disciplinary action if the student is found responsible (see Student Conduct Code for details). A student who has a course grade reduced by an instructor because of cheating or plagiarism, and who disputes the instructor's finding, may appeal the grade, but only by using the Course Grade Appeal Policy, which states that the student must prove the grade was arbitrary, prejudicial, or in error.

Unethical behavior in the academic setting includes, but is not limited to, cheating, plagiarism, and computer misuse, which are defined below:

The term "**cheating**" includes, but is not limited to:
- use of any unauthorized assistance in taking quizzes, tests, or examinations; or
- dependence upon the aid of sources beyond those authorized by the instructor in writing papers,
- preparing reports, solving problems, or carrying out other assignments; or
- the acquisition, without permission, of tests or other academic material belonging to a member of the
- University faculty or staff; or
- the advertisement, solicitation, or sale of term papers or research papers.-

The term "**plagiarism**" includes, but is not limited to:
- the use, by paraphrase or direct quotation, of the published or unpublished work of another person
- without full and clear acknowledgment; or
- the unacknowledged use of materials prepared by another person or agency engaged in the selling of
- term papers or other academic materials.

The term **"computer misuse"** is theft or other abuse of computer hardware, or software, including but not limited to Minnesota statues (609.87, 609.89):

- unauthorized entry into a file, to use, read, or change the contents, or for any other purpose; or
- unauthorized transfer of a file; or
- unauthorized use of another individual's identification and password; or
- use of computing facilities to interfere with the work of another student, faculty member, or
- University official; or
- use of computing facilities to send obscene or abusive messages; or
- use of computing facilities to interfere with normal operation of the University computing system; or
- theft or damage to computer equipment, software, electronic mail, or computer process.

(ENTER YOUR UNIVERSITY NAME)
SCHOOL OF BUSINESS INTEGRITY OATH
ACKNOWLEDGEMENT

In conjunction with my Application for Admission to the School of Business, I hereby acknowledge that I:
• have read the School of Business Integrity Oath; and
• agree to abide by its ethical behavior standards; and
• accept the consequences for failing to adhere to its ethical behavior standards.
I understand that my Application for Admission to the School of Business is conditional upon my agreement to abide by the ethical behavior standards set forth in the School of Business Integrity Oath.

_____
Signature

_____
Student Name

_____
Date

#2 Business School Code of Professionalism:
School of Business Code of Professionalism (What We Expect of Each Other)

Faculty, staff, and students in the School of Business at (Insert your university name) are expected to contribute to a culture of integrity and professionalism. Our School's culture encourages behaviors associated with educated and self-disciplined individuals. Those behaviors include:

- being honest;
- being reliable and prepared;
- being responsible for one's own actions and decisions; and
- being respectful of all individuals.

The Business School encourages the inclusion of this code at the top of each syllabus.

#3 Student Acknowledgement for the Course:

As an accounting student and someone considering entering the accounting profession, I believe in fostering an academic environment where competition is fair, integrity is promoted, and academic dishonesty is punished. As a member of this class, I voluntarily pledge my support for knowing and abiding by the University Academic Policies that exemplify ethical behavior in the academic setting.

#4 Student Acknowledgement for Individual Assignment:

The assignment turned in is solely the work of the student(s) signed below. Signing below acknowledges that no outside assistance has been obtained (for example - but not limited to - another current student in the course; a student who has taken this course in the past; a business professional; an accountant; an auditor; etc.). The only allowable assistance that may have been received is from your instructor and the campus writing center. Other than assistance from these two particular sources, all work on this assignment has been done by the student(s) signed below.

Typed   Name:_____

Signature:_____

Appendix B: Example of Cheating

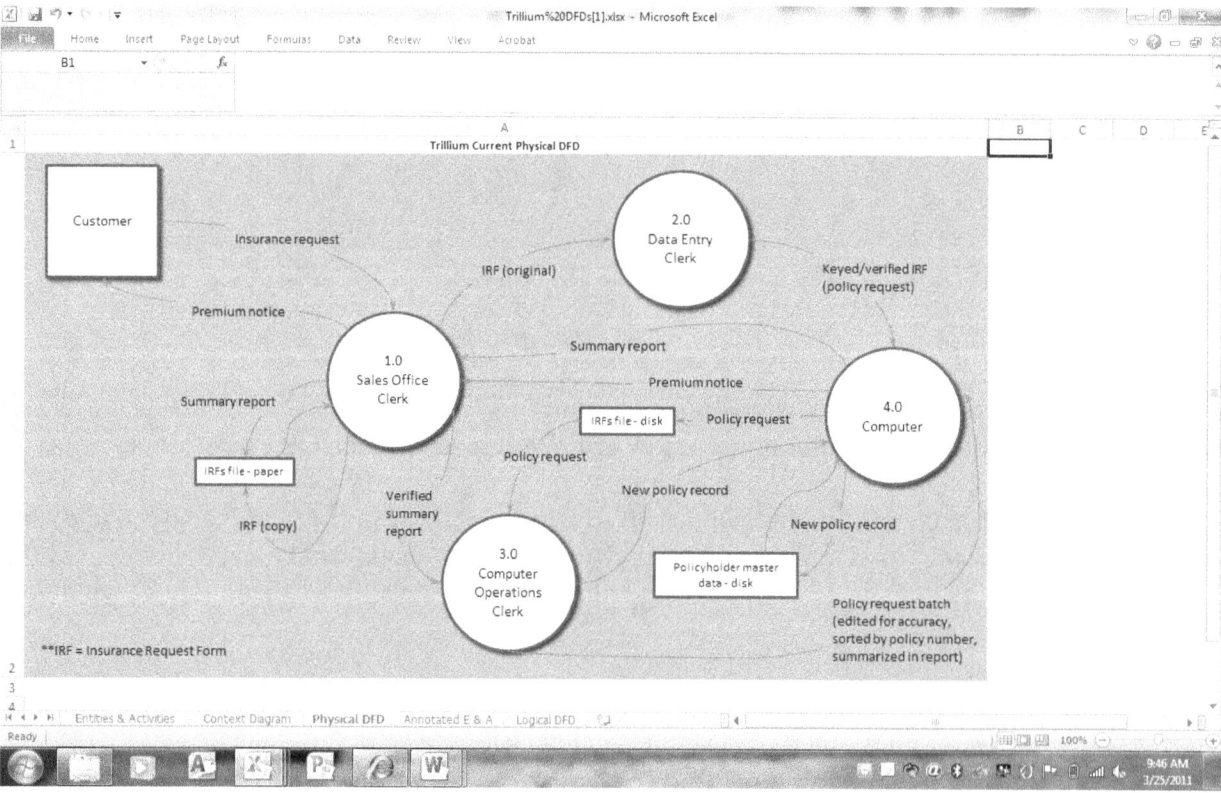

An Analysis of College Students' Perceptions of Workplace Bullying

Sue E. Joiner
Tarleton State University

Reggie R. Hall
Tarleton State University

Rickey E. Richardson
Tarleton State University

ABSTRACT

Workplace bullying has been defined as "Status-blind interpersonal hostility that is deliberate, repeated and sufficiently severe as to harm the targeted person's health or economic status" (Namie, 2003). This paper examines college students' perceptions of workplace bullying. To examine their perceptions, 200 participants completed an adaptation of the 2010 WBI U.S. Workplace Bullying Survey (Namie, 2010) containing demographic information, experience(s) with workplace bullying, and the implications of workplace bullying. As college students enter the professional workforce and become leaders in organizations, it is imperative they understand the challenges of workplace bullying. Internationally, specific legislation and a range of legal theories have been used to prevent and address workplace bullying. In the United States, specific legislation has yet to be passed, consequently recognized causes of action utilizing evidence of workplace bullying as contributing factors have been pursued in attempts at relief. Workplace bullying presents serious employee relation problems yet the concept remains silent in the realm of employee relations (Yamada, 2008).

Keywords: Workplace bullying, harassment, human resource management

Introduction

"Those that can, do; those who can't, bully!" (Harvey, Heames, Riches, & Leonard, 2006, p. 3). Workplace bullying continues to be the "hot topic" within businesses and organizations, yet these same businesses organizations are doing very little to stop the bullying. Harvey, Heames, Richey, and Leonard (2006), state that workplace bullying is shifting from the playground to the boardroom and offices in today's work environment. Organizations have been reluctant or may be unprepared to effectively deal with the issue of workplace bullying (Hall & Lewis, 2014). Although workplace bullying continues to present serious challenges to organizations, it remains one of the most ignored issues concerning employment relations (Yamada, 2008). Allowed to continue bullying can "work as an organizational cancer, eventually killing the entire firm" (Harvey, et al., 2006).

The purpose of this study is to examine college students' perceptions of workplace bullying. With permission from the Workplace Bullying Institute, an adaptation of its workplace bullying survey was administered to five undergraduate management classes and used to measure students' perceptions and experiences of being bullied and witnessing workplace bullying.

A brief review of workplace bullying, legislation and legal theories, and previous studies will be addressed in the next section. Measures and results of the workplace bullying survey will be discussed in the methodology section. Recommendations and conclusions for managers, leaders, employers, employees, and organizations to consider regarding workplace bullying in today's organizations will be the final section of this study.

Workplace Bullying Defined

Workplace bullying has been defined in literature numerous ways. Namie (2003), defined workplace bullying as "Status-blind interpersonal hostility that is deliberate, repeated and sufficiently severe as to harm the targeted person's health or economic status" (p. 1). Einarsen (1999) identified workplace bullying as repeated acts and practices, regardless of being deliberate or not, that affects job performance and creates a work environment that is undesirable, offensive and distressing to the victim. Bullies often distort the truth, blame others for their errors, and take credit for others' work (Cleary, Walter, & Robertson, 2009).

Vega and Comer (2005) used the term workplace bullying as the "pattern of destructive and generally deliberate demeaning of co-workers or subordinates that reminds us of the activities of the schoolyard bully" (p. 101). Additional theorists describe bullying at work as "repeated and persistent negative actions toward one or more individual(s), which involve a perceived power imbalance and create a hostile work environment" (Dhar, 2012, p. 80). Einarsen and Skogstad (1996) described this act as being difficult to defend oneself against actions by the perpetrator(s). Not surprising, these actions cause seriously strained relations among the perpetrator(s) and victim(s), which may very well spread throughout the entire organization.

Law and Legislation

Internationally, specific legislation and a range of legal theories have been used to prevent and address workplace bullying. In the United States specific legislation has yet to be passed, consequently recognized causes of action utilizing evidence of workplace bullying as contributing factors have been pursued in attempts at relief. Yamada (2010) states, "Despite the growing recognition of the harm caused by severe workplace bullying, many targets of this behavior have little recourse under law. Overall, workplace bullying remains the most neglected form of serious worker mistreatment in American employment law" (p. 253).

Attempts by countries other than the United States to prevent and remedy workplace bullying date back over 20 years in some cases. As a result, workers in some other developed countries have more protection from bullying than do their American counterparts. Sanders, Pattison and Bible (2012) observe:

> psychological abuse and bullying are also common in European countries, but they are being addressed through legislation. Europeans are more likely to provide remedies for actions that violate human dignity. Sweden, England, France, Germany, Italy, Spain, the Netherlands, Norway and parts of Canada and Australia have regulatory responses to workplace bullying. (p.3)

In addition to the countries listed above, some Brazilian states, Quebec, and other members of the European Union have laws against workplace bullying (Lippel, 2010; Bible, 2012; Sanders et al., 2012). Sweden, through legislation in 1993, has been reported as the first European nation to take a stand against bullying (Sanders et al., 2012). Most recently, in 2013, the Australian Federal Parliament enacted an amendment to its "Fair Work Act," effective January 1, 2014, which allows workers to seek help to stop bullying through the country's Fair Work Commission (Australia Fair Work Commission, 2013).

In the U.S. case of *Raess v. Doescher*, 883 N.E.2d 790, 794 (Ind. 2008), rehearing denied (June 30, 2008), the Indiana Supreme Court affirmed a trial court decision of a case which specifically included the term "workplace bullying" and arguably recognized the legitimacy of use of the term when characterizing a person's behavior. It should be noted however the Court did not recognize "workplace bullying" as an independent cause of action, but as part of the circumstances which in the case were germane to the claim of intentional infliction of emotional distress. Martin and LaVan (2010) observed, "even though there are no specific workplace bullying laws in the U.S., victims of workplace bullying can be legally protected" (p. 175).

Attempts at legal protection in the U.S. are typically pursued by coupling the hostile actions with other legal theories. Such theories include- assault, tortious interference with a business relationship, harassment (Title VII of the 1964 Civil Rights Act), Americans with Disabilities Act, constructive discharge, the Age Discrimination in Employment Act, Fair Labor Standards Act, Occupational Safety and Health Act, National Labor Relations Act, Labor Management Relations Act, Employee Retirement Income Security Act, Family and Medical Leave Act, Fair Credit Reporting Act, False Claims Act, Whistleblower Protection Act, and the First, Fourth, and Fourteenth Amendments(Bible, 2012; Sanders et al., 2012; Martin, Lopez & LaVan, 2009).

Legislatively, the Healthy Workplace Bill (HWB) and variations thereof have been the most concerted attempts in the United States to address workplace bullying. In 2004, the original version of the Bill authored by David Yamada was published (Yamada, 2010, p. 257). The Bill includes an independent cause of action for workplace bullying. Sanders et al. (2012) observed:
the key to application of the HWB cause of action is the existence of an abusive work environment or retaliation, both declared to be unlawful employment practices, which can be asserted against the employer on vicarious liability grounds and against an offending co-employee. (p.12)

Since its introduction, the Healthy Workplace Bill has been considered by over one-half of the State legislatures in the United States, but has failed to be enacted (Workplace Bullying Institute,

2014). Yamada (2010) writes "the concept of workplace bullying did not originate in America. Perhaps this is one reason why our legal system has lagged behind those of many other nations in providing more comprehensive responses to bullying at work" (p. 278). Even so, proponents of the Bill remain optimistic of eventual passage.

Workplace Bullying Surveys

Literature review and research on the issue of workplace bullying has been theoretical with few studies on actual bullying within organizations (Branch, Ramsay & Barker 2013). Drs. Gary and Ruth Namie are regarded as the authority on workplace bullying in North America. Gary, a social psychologist, and Ruth, a doctor of clinical psychology, have written numerous books and conducted surveys regarding workplace bullying. Together, they are considered to experts in their field. Gary Namie is currently the research director of Workplace Bullying Institute (WBI) and has published several surveys concerning workplace bullying. Currently, there are limited empirical studies concerning this topic from other sources.

In a survey conducted by the Workplace Bullying Institute (2010), 333 respondents stated only 4% of employers had broached awareness of workplace bullying, whereas 81% of employers did not stop the action. Of these, 46% were resistant to the topic of workplace bullying.

In 2012, WBI surveyed 311 employees asking them to identify written policies and procedures concerning workplace bullying in their organization. Surprisingly, limited policies and procedures covering workplace bullying were found with only 5.5% of employers having regulations and guidelines (WBI-2012-IP-B).

According to the WBI (2007) findings, 58% of bullying targets are women and 62% of perpetrators are men. Interestingly, in a survey conducted by the Workplace Bullying and Trauma Institute (Namie, 2000), the perpetrators were exactly 50% men and women alike which means they bully equally. Regarding gender, a 2000 study showed men and women are bullied approximately at the same rate. The WBI/Zogby survey found that 72 % of bullies are bosses and 55% of those bullied are rank-and-file workers (WBI/Zogby, 2007, p. 1).

Methodology

The purpose of this research is to examine workplace bullying as perceived by undergraduate college students. Within the literature most of the empirical studies have focused on the experiences of the traditional adult population. However, there is great importance in understanding and evaluating the perspectives of tomorrow's managers, employers, administrators, and employees. There is an expectation workplace bullying will increase, yet organizations have been hesitant and unprepared to effectively deal with the issue (Yamada, 2008). As discussed in the literature review, no specific legislation within the United States has been enacted to provide the necessary oversight prohibiting bullying within organizations.

Tomorrow's organizations must become more proactive in crafting policies and guidelines to prevent malicious and unintentional acts of bullying, whether such actions be physical, verbal or non-verbal. And, it is paramount to engage in practical applications of business and academic research that evaluates the perspectives and understanding of workplace bullying of our future professional workforce.

A survey consisting of 10 questions was administered to undergraduate students at a regional university in the southern United States. The survey instrument utilized was an adaptation of the 2010 Workplace Bullying Institute Survey by Dr. Namie and was used with permission of Dr. Namie and the Workplace Bullying Institute. The survey items have been used and commissioned by Zogby International, as online (non-scientific) surveys and two national scientific surveys. The 10 questions were administered to students enrolled in undergraduate business courses. The course sections chosen for this study were selected as a convenience sample based on the courses currently being taught by the second author. The sections chosen included three sections of Principles of Management and two sections of Fundamentals of Human Resource Management. Two of the three sections are online instruction-based courses. Students enrolled within the courses consisted of various academic majors across the university, with the vast majority classified at the junior or senior levels. There were 100 responses and students were provided extra credit for their participation.

Results

Basic descriptive statistics were utilized to evaluate the college students' perceptions on workplace bullying. Questions included multiple-choice options ranging from two to seven options on specified questions.

Descriptive statistics were generated for all 10 questions. The sample size and percentages were collected for each question within this study. Table 2 displays the descriptive data for the 10 questions included within the survey. The descriptive research will not attempt to indicate causal relationships, but is intended to provide more insight on existing research and perceptions of bullying within the workplace.

Table 1: Experience with workplace bullying

What is your experience with workplace bullying? (Question 1)	N	%
I was bullied before but not now, and have witnessed.	31	31%
I have never been personally bullied, but have witnessed other bullies.	55	55%
I have never been bullied, never witnessed it and never been a bully.	6	6%

According to the results from the 2010 WBI Survey, 35% of adult workers acknowledged being bullied at work, which extrapolated would equate to over 50 million Americans and over 15% admitted witnessing workplace bullying (WBI, 2010). In our survey, 31% of college students admitted to being bullied within the workplace but are not being bullied currently. Over half (55%) of the participants admitted to having never been bullied personally, but have witnessed bullying activities within the workplace.

Table 2: Demographics of Participants

Which category below includes your gender and age? (Question 2)	N	%
Female between ages of 18-21	39	39
Female between ages of 22-25	10	10
Female 25 or older	14	14
Male between ages of 18-21	17	17
Male between ages of 22-25	9	9
Male 25 or older	11	11

Table 2 reflects the demographic characteristics of the 100 undergraduate students participating within the research. Sixty three percent of the participants were female undergraduates. Of the participants, 39% were females between the ages of 18-21. Ten percent of the participants were females between the ages of 22-25 and 14% were 25 or older. Seventeen percent of the participants were males ranging between the ages 18-21. Of the remaining participants, 9% were males between the ages of 22-25 and 11% were 25 years of age or older. Twenty five percent of the total number of participants would be categorized as non-traditional students.

Table 3: Gender of the Bullying Targets

What is the gender of the person targeted for mistreatment (workplace bullying)? (Question 3)	N	%
Female	63	64.29
Male	35	35.71

The 2010 WBI survey found 58% of targets are women. The results from our replicated study indicated similar findings. The survey found 64% of targets of workplace bullying are women. With women expected to comprise close to half of the U.S. labor force (47%) these findings are worthy of more investigation (Bureau of Labor Statistics Reports, 2013).

Table 4: Gender of the Perpetrator

What was the gender of the principal perpetrator and their rank relative to the targeted person (you, if you were the target? *(Question 4)*	N	%
Female and ranked higher than target	24	24.49

	N	%
Female and ranked lower than target	7	7.14
Female and the same rank as the target	19	19.39
Male and ranked higher than target	28	28.57
Male and ranked lower than target	5	5.10
Male and the same rank as the target	15	15.31

Table 5: Perpetrators' Supporters

Who supported (helped) the perpetrator, if anyone? (Check all that apply) *(Question 5)*	N	%
No one	43	44.79
The target's peers	23	23.96
The perpetrator's peers	26	27.08
Human resources	3	3.13
One or more senior managers or senior administrators	14	14.58

Table 6. Forms of Workplace Bullying

Describe the forms of mistreatment. Check all that apply. *(Question 6)*	N	%
Verbal abuse (e.g. yelling, belittling, name calling, malicious sarcasm, threats to safety	74	74
Intimidation (e.g. public or	61	61

private, actions that were threatening, humiliating, hostile, offensive, cruel		
Interference with work performance (e.g. sabotage, undermining, ensuring failure	45	45
Abuse of authority (e.g. misuse of performance appraisal, creating a fearful work environment)	38	38
Destruction of Workplace Relationships (e.g. with co-workers, bosses or customers, icing out workers)	34	34
Retaliation (e.g. for filing a complaint or testifying).	16	16

Table 6. Forms of Workplace Bullying

Describe the forms of mistreatment. Check all that apply. *(Question 6)*	N	%
Verbal abuse (e.g. yelling, belittling, name calling, malicious sarcasm, threats to safety	**74**	**74**
Intimidation (e.g. public or private, actions that were threatening, humiliating, hostile, offensive, cruel	**61**	**61**
Interference with work performance (e.g. sabotage, undermining, ensuring failure	**45**	**45**
Abuse of authority (e.g. misuse of performance appraisal, creating a fearful work environment)	**38**	**38**
Destruction of Workplace Relationships (e.g. with co-workers, bosses or customers, icing out workers)	**34**	**34**
Retaliation (e.g. for filing a complaint or testifying).	**16**	**16**

Table 6. Forms of Workplace Bullying

Describe the forms of mistreatment. Check all that apply. (Question 6)	N	%
Verbal Abuse (e.g. yelling, belittling, name calling, malicious sarcasm, threats to safety)	74	74
Intimidation (e.g. public or private, actions that were threatening, humiliating, hostile, offensive, cruel)	61	61
Interference with work performance (e.g. sabotage, underminining, ensuring failure)	45	45
Abuse of authority (e.g. misuse of performance appraisal, creating a fearful work environment)	38	38
Destruction of Workplace Relationships (e.g. with co-workers, bosses or customers, icing out workers)	34	34
Retaliation (e.g. for filing a complaint or testifying). Retaliation (e.g. for filing a complaint or testifying).Retaliation (e.g. for filing a complaint or testifying)	16	16

Table 7: Mistreatment Implications

Did the mistreatment result in stress-related health complications: psychological or physical for the targeted person? (Question 7)	N	%
Yes	17	17
No	35	35
Not sure	48	48

College students acknowledged 35% of the workplace bullying observed was peer-to-peer bullying. The WBI survey found 53% of the perpetrators of bullying, were ranked higher than the target of bullying regardless of the gender of the perpetrator. The results are expressed in more detail in Table 4. "A pre-existing or evolved imbalance of power between the parties is considered central to the bullying experience, as this may limit targets' ability to retaliate or successfully defend themselves" (Einarsen, Hoel, & Notelaers, 2011). Interestingly, men and women are essentially equal participants in their execution of bullying, 49% and 51% respectively. Table 5 displays the results from Question 5 which asked: Who supported (helped) the perpetrator, if anyone? Forty-four percent of the perpetrators operated solo in their bullying efforts. Perpetrators were corroborated by their peers (27%) or the target's peers (24%).

Table 8: Stopping the Mistreatment

What action did the targeted individual undertake to stop the mistreatment? (Question 8)	N	%
Filed a formal complaint with human resources, senior management or owner	12	12.24
Filed a formal discrimination complaint with an external state or federal agency	0	0
Filed a lawsuit in court	1	1.02
Complained informally to the employer by telling management, no formal complaint	35	35.71
Took no action, either formal or informal	35	35.71
Not sure	15	15.31

More than 35% of participants indicated recipients of bullying failed to take formal or informal action. Another 35% complained informally to their employer but failed to file a formal complaint. While Namie (2007) found British employees are hesitant (11%) to report bullying issues to organizations. Only 1% of respondents in this study indicated the target had filed a lawsuit in court. The low percentage may be indicative of the non-existent U.S. laws that specifically prohibit workplace bullying. In contrast, most European nations have laws which prohibit bullying behaviors (Namie, 2007).

Table 9: Mistreatment Consequences

When the mistreatment was reported what did the employer do? (Question 9)	N	%
Employer did nothing; target eventually lost job, perpetrator was retained and/or promoted	21	21
Employer did nothing; target was retaliated against for reporting the mistreatment but kept job	8	8
Employer did nothing; complaint was ignored, no negative consequences for either party	38	38

Conducted investigation; concluded no wrongdoing, target was retaliated against	11	11
Conducted investigation; concluded wrongdoing, negative consequences for perpetrator.	22	22

Table 10: Remedy for the Mistreatment

What stopped the mistreatment? (Check one) (Question 10)	N	%
It has not stopped.	19	19
Mistreatment has stopped, and perpetrator was terminated	10	10
Mistreatment stopped and perpetrator stayed but was punished	24	24
Mistreatment stopped and target transferred within the organization	7	7
Mistreatment stopped and target voluntarily left the organization	27	27
Mistreatment stopped and target was terminated, driven out of the organization	13	13

College student participants indicated that in most cases (67%) when the mistreatment was reported, the employer did nothing. Twenty-one percent indicated that adverse employment actions occurred to the target and the perpetrator remained employed with the company. The survey findings also suggested that 38% of the reported incidents were ignored and no negative consequences were issued for either target or perpetrator.   Twenty-two percent of the students reported organizations investigated the action. However, adverse employment actions did not result for the perpetrator.   Table 10 displays the results from question 10 which inquired: What stopped the mistreatment? Forty percent of participants reported mistreatment stopped as result of either the target voluntarily leaving the organization (27%) or being terminated by the organization (13%). On a more positive note, 34% of participants indicated the mistreatment stopped and the perpetrator was either terminated (10%) or punished (24%).

Limitations Limitations

The study uses a convenience sample of undergraduate students. Undergraduate students may have limited professional work experiences. Two of the sections selected in the study were 100% online courses that may have consisted of more non-traditional students. Non-traditional students are those students 25 years of age or older (Pelletier, 2010) and may have different perspectives based upon the likelihood of more work experience.

Recommendations

Workplace bullying has implications affecting the organizational culture, employee morale, quality of work-life, and well-being of employees. Organizational cultures should foster an environment of civility and respect. According to Cleary et al. (2009), "Healthy workplaces are ones in which leaders and managers lead by example, champion respect, and set the tone and expectation for behaviors essential for fostering a harmonious and collaborative environment. The role of the leader/manager is crucial in developing a positive workplace culture that supports a high level of professionalism and a culture of zero tolerance toward bullying." (p. 34).

Every manager possesses a bases of power but those who utilize each facet will be more effective in the creation of the utopian work environment for employees resulting in more profitability and reducing the unnecessary costs associated with stress, hypertension and disengaged employees (Hall & Lewis, 2014).

Over 80% of students participating in this study reported personally experiencing or witnessing workplace bullying. However, these students indicated there is rarely any adverse employment action taken by the employer. Women are expected to comprise close to half of the U.S. labor force (47%) yet experience over 60% of bullying incidents (Bureau of Labor Statistics Reports, 2013). These figures require further investigation. Currently in the United States, no legislation exist specifically prohibiting workplace bullying, so there appears to be a likelihood bullying will continue. If passed legislation, such as the Healthy Workplace Bill may provide more protection to employees.

The researchers propose four basic strategies to remedy workplace bullying within organization: (1) communication of policies and implications to all employees, (2) remain aware of organizational policies and the current work environment, (3) listen to employees and other stakeholders to understand the organizational climate, and (4) lead the way by providing specific workplace behaviors in all types of communication (Hall & Lewis, 2014).

References

2014   WBI.   How   Bullying   Happens.   http://www.workplacebulyng.org/individuals/problem/how-bullying-happens/

2013   WBI-Zogby   Workplace   Bullying   from   the   Perspective   of   U.S.   Business   Leaders. http://workplacebullying.org/multi/pdf/2013-WBI-Z-BL.pdf

2010   WBI   U.S.   Workplace   Bullying   Survey.   Http://www.workplacebullying.org/research/WBI-NatlSurvey2010.html

Australia Fair Work Commission (2013, December 31). *Anti-bullying.* Retrieved from http://www.fwc.gov.au/index.cfm?pagename=anti-bullying

Bible, J. D. (2012). The jerk at work: Workplace bullying and the law's inability to combat it. *Employee Relations Law Journal, 38*(1), 32-51.

Branch, S., Ramsay, S, & Barker, M. (2013). Workplace bullying, mobbing and general harassment: A review. *International Journal of Management Reviews*. 15, 280-299.

Bureau of Labor Statistics (2013) *Women in the labor force: A Databook*. 1-104.

Cleary, M., Hunt, G. E., Walter, G., & Robertson, M. (2009). Dealing with bullying in the workplace: Toward zero tolerance. *Journal of Psychosocial Nursing & Mental Health Services 47*(12), 34-41.

Dhar, R. L. (2012). Why do they bully? Bullying behavior and its implication on the bullied. *Journal of Workplace Behavioral Health, 27*, 79-99. doi:10.1080/15555240.2012.666463

Einarsen, S., Hoel, H, & Notelaers, G. (2009) Measuring exposure to bullying and harassment at work: Validity, factor structure and psychometric properties of the Negative Acts Questionnaire-Revised. *Work & Stress*, 23: 24-44.

Einarsen, S. & Skogstad, A. (1996). Bullying at work: Epidemiological findings in public and private organizations. *European Journal of Work and Organizational Psychology, 5,* 185- 201.

Hall, R., & Lewis, S. (2014). Managing workplace bullying and social media policy: Implications for employee engagement. *Academy of Business Research Journal, I,* 128- 138.

Harvey, M. G., Heames, J. T., Richey, R. Gl, & Leonard, N. (2006). Bullying: From the playground to the boardroom. *Journal of Leadership and Organizational Studies, 12*(4), 1-11.

Lim, V.K.G. and Teo, T.S.H. (2009). Mind your E-Manners: Impact of cyber incivility on employees' work attitude and behavior. *Information & Management* 46 (2009), 419-425.

Lippel, K. (2010). The law of workplace bullying: An international overview. *Comparative Labor Law & Policy Journal, 32*(1), 1-13.

Martin, W. & LaVan, H. (2010). Workplace bullying: A review of litigated cases. *Employee Responsibilities and Rights Journal, 22*(3), 175-194.

Martin, W. N., Lopez, Y. P. & LaVan, H.N. (2009). What legal protections do victims of bullies in the workplace have? *Journal of Workplace Rights, 14*(2), 143-156.

Namie, G. (2003). Workplace bullying: Escalated incivility. *Ivey Business Journal, 68,* 1-6.

Namie, G. (2000). U. S. hostile workplace survey. Retrieved from www.workplacebully.org/ Multi/pdf/N-N-2000.pdf.

Pelletier, S.G. (2010). Success for Adult Students. *Public Purpose. 1-6.*

Raess v. Doescher, 883 N.E.2d 790, 794 (Ind. 2008), rehearing denied (June 30, 2008).

Sanders, D. E., Pattison, P. & Bible, J.D. (2012). Legislating "nice": Analysis and assessment of proposed workplace bullying prohibitions. *Southern Law Journal, 22*(1), 1-36.

Vega, G. & Comer, D. R. (2005). Sticks and stones may break your bones, but words can break   your spirit: Bullying in the workplace. *Journal of Business Ethics, 58,* 101-109. Doi: 10.1007/s10551-005-1422-7

Workplace Bullying Institute (2014). *Healthy Workplace Bill.* Retrieved from
        http://www.healthyworkplacebill.org/about.php

Yamada, D.C. (2010). Workplace bullying and American employment law: A Ten-Year progress
        report and assessment. *Comparative Labor Law & Policy Journal, 32*(Fall), 251-280.

Yamada, D.C. (2008). Workplace bullying and ethical leadership. *Journal of Values-Based Leadership.*
        1(2), 49-62.

Rickey E. Richardson, CPA, J.D., Ph.D. is assistant professor of business law in the College of Business Administration at Tarleton State University. His research and teaching interests focus on the regulation of business.

Sue Joiner, EdD is an Assistant Professor in the College of Business at Tarleton State University. Her teaching interests are administrative systems, general business, and marketing. Dr. Joiner's research interests are vocational business education.

Reggie Hall, PHR, EdD is an Assistant Professor in the Management Department in the College of Business at Tarleton State University. He also serves as the Coordinator for Mentoring Programs for the Office of Diversity and Inclusion at Tarleton. His research interests include human resource issues and employee engagement.

Resurrecting Shared Governance:
A Model to Face Uncertain Times in Higher Education

Sharon Beaudry
Colby-Sawyer College

Elizabeth Crockford
Colby-Sawyer College

ABSTRACT

Most private higher educational institutions were founded upon Harvard's shared governance model, in which faculty plays a significant role in decision making in the areas of academic policy and personnel. In 1980, due to this shared governance approach, the Supreme Court determined under NLRB v. Yeshiva, that faculty at private institutions were management and not eligible to bargain collectively under the National Labor Relations Act. However, over time private institutions have been under increasing economic and political pressure to make operational changes that have led to a deterioration of shared governance structures at some institutions, significantly lessening the role of faculty in decision-making for the institution.

While changes to shared governance can have both positive and negative consequences for faculty and administrators, this trend has inadvertently opened many colleges to unionization efforts among faculty. This paper will provide an overview of the history of shared governance and its underlying legal precedence; the benefits and drawbacks of shared governance; and a comparative analysis of resources expended in shared governance versus unionization efforts. Finally, we provide a comprehensive model that may aid faculty and administration in reenergizing shared governance structures for the long-term benefit of the institution.

Keywords: shared faculty governance, faculty unionization, Yeshiva doctrine

Introduction

Most private higher educational institutions were founded upon a shared governance model in which faculty plays a significant role in decision making in the areas of academic policy and personnel. In 1980, due to this shared governance approach, the Supreme Court determined that Yeshiva University faculty were management and not eligible to bargain collectively under the National Labor Relations Act (NLRB v. Yeshiva, 1980). Since this decision, many colleges have avoided unionization among their faculty. However, over time private institutions have been under increasing economic and political pressure to make operational changes that have led to a deterioration of shared governance structures, significantly lessening the role of faculty in decision-making at some institutions (Hansmann, 2012). While doing so, they have inadvertently opened greater interest in faculty unionization today than in years past.

Today, unionization among small private institutions is still minimal, however, the erosion of shared governance may create a sense of a lost voice, and unions could present a viable alternative not previously considered by small private faculty. Unfortunately, for both faculty and administration, the cost of this alternative, financially, philosophically, and economically, exceeds that of enhancing current shared governance systems, or creating one if none now exists.

This paper will provide an overview of the history of shared governance and its underlying legal precedence; the benefits and drawbacks of shared governance; and a comparative analysis of resources expended in shared governance versus unionization. Finally, we provide a comprehensive model that may aid faculty and administration in reenergizing shared governance structures for the long-term benefit of the institution and its stakeholders.

Background

The Shared Governance Model

At the heart of union-avoidance strategy is the shared governance model, which is widely employed by private colleges and universities. According to the American Federation of Teachers (2006): "Shared governance is the set of practices under which college faculty and staff participate in significant decisions concerning the operation of their institutions" (p. 4). Unique to higher education, this management model had its beginnings in the 19th century, when Harvard University faculty became increasingly dissatisfied with decisions made by the governing board and president, which had sole authority at the time (Jones, 2011). After years of dissention and debate, in 1826 Harvard created a new shared governance model, which gave faculty, due to their disciplinary expertise, control over admissions, instruction and discipline (Jones, 2011). Thereafter, this model was adopted by private institutions throughout the United States (Jones, 2011).

Legal Influences

Prior to 1980, the National Labor Relations Board routinely found faculty to be non-managerial employees, thereby not subject to collective bargaining (Metchick & Sigh, 2004). However, when the faculty union of Yeshiva University won a union election, the University challenged the unionization efforts (NLRB v. Yeshiva, 1980). After several appeals, the case was heard by the Supreme Court.

The Supreme Court, in a five to four decision, ruled for the University (NLRB v. Yeshiva, 1980). Specifically, the Court found that the Yeshiva faculty exercised nearly complete authority in academic matters, and also held substantial authority in non-academic matters such as academic personnel (NLRB v. Yeshiva, 1980). In its decision, the Court compared the collaborative decision making process of faculty to a traditional industrial structure in determining this managerial role. "To the extent the industrial analogy applies, the faculty determine … the product to be produced, the terms upon which it will be offered, and the customers who will be served" (NLRB v. Yeshiva, 1980, para. 43). Due to the court decision determining that shared governance bestows management status on their faculty, the university was free to refuse recognition of the union (NLRB v. Yeshiva, 1980).

Following this decision, the NLRB's General Counsel issued new guidelines for evaluating bargaining unit status of faculty for private institutions, which is still in place today. These standards can be divided into two categories, both of which must be met for faculty to be considered management and exempt from the National Labor Relations Act:

- **Academic educational policies**. Faculty should have decision-making authority over curriculum (course content, schedules, textbooks), teaching loads, grading systems and policies, admissions policies, graduation policies (including degree requirements), teaching methods and class size (Metchick & Sigh, 2004).

- **Academic personnel policies**. Faculty should also have decision-making authority over faculty hiring, evaluations, tenure, retention, promotions and sabbaticals policies (Metchick & Sigh, 2004).

This standard, known as the Yeshiva doctrine, effectively bars faculty bodies from unionizing. The NLRB considers each situation on a case-by-case basis, and considers the level of control or authority that faculty have over these decisions (Metchick & Sigh, 2004). In other words, if the faculty makes recommendations, but they are often dismissed by the administration in favor of alternative decisions, or there is a lack of consultation, then the faculty does not have authority. However, if nearly all recommendations made by faculty are upheld by the administration, then authority is present and the faculty is considered management.

Shifts from Shared Governance

Economic Challenges

Over the course of the last decade, higher education within the United States has been undergoing significant economic and political pressures (Hansmann, 2012). The cost of tuition continues to increase by about 5 percent per year and the student loan default rate is over 20 percent (White, 2013). With private donations falling and less government-funded support than in previous decades, higher education is under pressure to find solutions to the student debt crisis (White, 2013). Moreover, increasing shifts to for-profit colleges, offering on-line education to greater numbers of students, is impacting the market of traditional private residential colleges (Hansmann, 2012).

Due to these numerous factors, institutions are under pressure to cut costs to remain viable. This has led to institutions cutting programs that are not profitable, while expanding into new, more profitable ventures that move beyond traditional academia (Hansmann, 2012). Additionally, the industry has seen significant increases in the use of part-time adjunct faculty and the reduction of tenure-eligible faculty positions (Hansmann, 2012). These economic challenges and cost cutting measures have been a substantial factor in the shifts seen in shared governance. Administrators are often forced to bypass the shared governance structure in favor of more swift, business-driven decisions. This has included issues of curriculum and faculty personnel, which circuitously leads to even weaker governance structures.

Consequences of Shifts from Shared Governance

Advantages: The advantages to faculty and the institution of a reduction in shared governance are few, though critical. They include:

- *Adaptability.* As early as the 1980s, George Keller was critical of faculty's inability to adapt to the economic realities being foreshadowed (1983). Keller proposed that governance was becoming less about faculty involvement for the greater good of the institution, but rather individuals protecting their own disciplines and self-interest in a new reality which witnessed the discontinuation of programs that were no longer economically viable or relevant (Keller, 1983). It was administrators who saw the need to adapt and change with the times.

- *Speed of Decision Making.* According to Crellin (2010), faculty governance is often criticized for the lack of efficiency in decision-making. As a result, some institutions have brought in non-academic leaders who adopt swift, for-profit management methods. For example, Wesleyan University was one of the first to hire a non-academic investment banker who employed significant cost-cutting measures to turn around the institution's financial crisis. The new management publically proclaimed that they no longer would adhere to the old bottom-up approach, since they needed to move swiftly to manage the challenges (Keller, 1983). While authority in traditional academic matters has remained in some areas, issues such as student body size, tuition costs, location and budgets, now often resides with centralized administration models (Jaschick, 2012).

- *Operational Effectiveness.* Administrators have recognized the need to expand revenue streams for operational effectiveness. According to Gerber (2014), while some institutions have been successful in shifting to a more strategic governance approach involving faculty, most schools have been generally ineffective in this switch. Therefore, administrators find they need to bypass faculty involvement when adopting new non-tradition programs, such as online offerings, in order to compete in today's environment.

Disadvantages: While advantages may occur when there are fewer voices at the table, shutting out faculty from governance issues results in considerable drawbacks:

- *Fewer Faculty involved in Governance.* According to Gerber (2014), whereas in earlier decades, part-time faculty only equated to 30 percent, by 2011, 75 percent of all college instructors were either part-time adjuncts, graduate assistants or in non-tenured eligible positions. This dramatic shift has resulted in significantly less involvement in governance, both by tenured faculty who are asked to do more, and part-time faculty who are not expected or invited to participate. While at one time, institutions recognized the quality of their "product" was managed by faculty, today's de-professionalism of faculty may be impacting that quality.

- *Poor Morale.* This de-professionalism has led to an unbundling of faculty work, lower pay, poor working conditions, lack of office space and institutional support for instructors, not to mention a lack of connection to the institution as a whole (Gerber, 2014). This results in poor morale by faculty seeking a way to find a voice – which seemingly points to unionization as more attractive in this atmosphere.

- *Unionization.* Unlike other industries that have witnessed a drop in union membership, higher education has seen an increase among faculty. According to data collected by the National Center for the Study of Collective Bargaining in Higher Education, the increase from 2006 to 2012 of union members in this sector rose by 14 percent (Berry, J & Savarese, M., 2012). Concerns surrounding the political climate, eroding numbers of tenure-eligible, full-time faculty positions, and college governance have played a role in attracting unionization (Riley, 2011). This does not even reflect the current trend of union organizers targeting adjunct faculty and even graduate teaching assistants.

- *Associated Union Costs.* Within the higher education industry, there is strong evidence that unionization does lead to higher compensation (Thornton & Curtis, 2012). According to the 2011-12 AAUP's Annual Report of Economic Status of the Profession, unionized faculty earn an average of seven to 16 percent more than non-union faculty (Thornton & Curtis, 2012). It is also not uncommon that when one bargaining unit gains higher wages, employers will extend the negotiated wage and benefit increases to non-unionized workers in order to avoid further unionization (Fossum, 2012). Moreover, unionization has historically brought on a host of inflexible work rules that can have a negative impact upon productivity and decision-making (Fossum, 2012). Table 1 is provided to show the salary and benefits cost differential comparing a unionized verses non-unionized faculty body of 100 members, which equates to $900,000 annually.

There are several cases showing significant changes in the shared governance structure at American colleges and universities. For example, in 2004, Point Park University's faculty challenged their right to unionize after the administration made changes to the faculty handbook without consulting faculty. The initial determination by the National Labor Relations Board (NLRB) was that the faculty could form a union and were not considered management (Point Park University, 2012). Following an overruled decision in 2006 by the appeals court, many believe that the NLRB is now poised to develop new criteria, departing from the Yeshiva doctrine, in the wake of changes to the shared governance systems, opening private institutions to unionization (Westcott, 2012).

A Solution for Mutual Benefit

While shared governance has some drawbacks in a fast-paced, dynamic industry, it has many more benefits and its overall direct costs are considerably lower than a unionized faculty. While a large institution can absorb the costs of unionized segments of faculty (full time and adjunct alike), smaller, tuition-dependent private colleges are not so immune to the financial and other harm a unionized faculty might cause. It is in the best interest of the small private college, its leadership, faculty, students, and other stakeholders to avoid unionization in favor of returning to vibrant and healthy shared governance.

Overriding Strategy

Some of the overriding strategic themes in achieving a working model include:

- **Leadership and Collaboration.** To enact this plan, it is important to begin with an initial review of the problem with senior administrators to ensure buy-in. Without their understanding of an institution's cost/benefit reality regarding shared governance versus the potential for unionization, any plan undertaken will only be short-lived. Starting with leadership, the long-term goal is to ensure all parties involved in shared governance are maintaining the standards established within the process. Rather than dueling perspectives, institutional leaders need to create a culture of shared challenges, embracing the need for a high quality product to be delivered in the most efficient and effective manner; one that is competitively priced and affordable. Faculty and administrators need to come together under a veil of common trust to solve these challenges together, which may involve a significant change from long-held – or maybe newly employed - practices.

- **Gain Internal Support**. Internal marketing to employees is essential for a successful outcome. While most faculty bodies would likely embrace the idea of an increased shared governance process, within an institution that lacks trust, faculty may initially be skeptical. This process can begin with institutional leaders discussing the importance of a shared governance approach for the betterment of the institution. Ng (2012) recommends seeking out several respected employees to give them a chance to evaluate the idea of a governance review process. Within the college environment, these opinion leaders would include department chairs, along with several active and well-respected faculty members who can serve as initial ambassadors to communicate the need for this process.

- **Cost Considerations**. For a small to midsized private college, the total direct and indirect cost of the review process is estimated at $32,000. Table 2 outlines the details of these costs. Most of this includes indirect personnel costs associated with reviewing the governance practices, as well as the committee audit work. Some funds are needed to cover the direct costs of attorney fees. As noted previously, the cost of refocusing an institution's shared governance system compares favorably to the estimated $900,000 annual estimated cost of unionization.

Plan of Action

The proposed solution requires a three-stage process as follows, also presented in abbreviated form in Table 3:

1. **Initial Review**. The first stage involves an initial review of the current governance structure by the chief human resources officer and outside legal counsel. This process should compare the current documents, such as the faculty handbook and other governance documents, with the Yeshiva doctrine (Metchick & Sigh, 2004). Moreover, a preliminary examination of decisions that have occurred within the last few years would establish the rate at which administrators implement faculty recommendations (Metchick & Sigh, 2004). The findings should then be presented to the college's president, chief academic officer, as well as other officers and trustees whose role would involve academic-related governance. This process should take about two months.

2. **Governance review committee**. The second stage of the process comprises a committee to be charged with a review of the current status of shared governance within the institution. The committee should utilize the American Association of University Professors (AAUP) governance guidance documents, as well as best practices of other institutions (Ramo, 2001). Moreover, the committee will need to be made aware of any findings of apparent deficiencies with the Yeshiva doctrine so these gaps might be addressed. This process should take nine months to a year.

   - *Committee makeup*. The committee should include a broad range of participants from all areas of institutional governance. This might include trustees, senior officers or deans from the academic area, as well as faculty of various rank and disciplines (Ramo, 2001). In some cases, students and staff may also be included depending on the culture and structure of governance within the institution.

   - *Survey*. The committee may want to initially begin with assessing the perceptions of the current shared governance process of the various stakeholders. The AAUP has a prepared questionnaire for this purpose entitled *Indicators of Sound Governance*, which should be considered as a basis for evaluating the current status (Ramo, 2001). This instrument measures opinions related to three areas: (1) curriculum, instruction and research; (2) matters of faculty status including hiring, retention, tenure and promotion; and (3) the aspects of student life that relate to the educational process (Ramo, 2001).

   - *Definition of shared governance and statement of committee purpose*. The committee will then develop a definition of shared governance for the institution, as well as a purpose for the committee. This should be initially established by the committee and then reviewed by the various stakeholder groups.

   - *Audit of shared governance processes*. The committee will then proceed to audit the work and procedures of various standing committees that involve governance issues. This would include a review of the structure of the committee, procedures, committee make-up and the means by which the full faculty is involved in final decisions (Governance Working Group, 2012). This audit process should also seek to review the results of recommendations of faculty committees and the rate at which they have been implemented by administrators.

- *Recommendations*. Once the audit work has been completed, the committee should then develop means by which the shared governance process may be strengthened. This may involve updated committee procedures that ensure all faculty are involved in decision-making. These should be presented to all stakeholders.

- *Implementation and follow-up*. The committee is finally charged with the implementation of approved recommendations. This stage might also reassess the opinions of the various stakeholders. While this process may be a one-time working group, some institutions may develop a standing committee that provides oversight of shared governance issues on an ongoing basis.

3. **Final Review**. Once the initial work of the governance committee is complete, it will be necessary for an additional review of the updated procedures in light of the Yeshiva doctrine. Once again, this would require an examination by the chief human resources officer and legal counsel. If there are gaps that have not been addressed, these should be forwarded to the governance committee for follow up. Once again, this review process should take two months to complete.

While this three-stage process is critical to understand the current status of shared governance model within an institution, over time it needs to be monitored and reviewed to maintain its strength. Using the model above helps ensure compliance with the Yeshiva doctrine, which would have the direct effect of barring any unionization attempts. While the timeline here is relatively extensive, initial efforts should pacify both administration and faculty that the outcome is worth the investment of time and energy on all fronts. Administration should be willing to support the work necessary to gain an outcome that will reduce costs and the threat of unionization, while faculty will begin to see the results of regaining a voice and become ever-more committed to the outcome as the benefits of a clear and vigorous shared governance system grow clearer and more realistic.

Areas for future development in the revitalization of shared governance include a focus on how part-time faculty can play a more extensive role in shared governance to avoid the rising trend of unionism within that segment. Moreover, a comparative analysis of different shared governance structures could be studied to ascertain the amount of true management involvement of faculty at all levels and ranks under those models in order to develop similar plans to address those specific needs.

Conclusion

Faculty input in the areas of governance is a long held tradition in academia. The deterioration of shared governance with faculty has resulted in a disenfranchised faculty who may look elsewhere to seek the voice that has been diminished. One of these alternatives is unionization. The cost of a faculty labor union is prohibitive to small private institutions – already experiencing economic challenges. We have presented a model useful to those institutions who wish to restructure, recreate, or simply redraft their own shared governance models. The legal framework of the Yeshiva doctrine and the huge cost of either fighting a unionization effort by faculty – or accepting a labor union should be strong incentive for leadership to willingly seek to reinstate a strong faculty governance model that in itself creates a barrier to potential costly unionization in the future.

Resources

2012-13 Administrators in higher education salary survey. College and University Professional Association for Human Resources. Retrieved from http://www.cupahr.org/surveys/files/salary2013/AHE13-Executive-Summary.pdf

2013-13 Faculty in higher education salary survey. College and University Professional Association for Human Resources. Retrieved from http://www.cupahr.org/surveys/files/salary2013/FHE4-2013-Executive-Summary.pdf

American Federation of Teachers. (2006). Shared governance in colleges and universities: A statement by the higher education program and policy council. Retrieved from: www.aft.org/pubs-reports/higher_ed/shared_governance.pdf.

Berry, J & Savarese, M. (2012). Directory of U.S. faculty contracts and bargaining agents in institutions of higher education. National Center for the Study of Collectivity Bargaining in Higher Education and the Professions. Retrieved from http://www.insidehighered.com/sites/default/server_files/files/facdirectory.pdf

Burdge, R. (2011). United States attorney fee survey report 2010-2011. Retrieved from http://www.nclc.org/images/pdf/litigation/fee-survey-report-2010-2011.pdf

Crellin, M. A. (2010). The future of shared governance. *New Directions For Higher Education*, (151), 71-81. doi:10.1002/he.402.

Fossum, J. (2012). *Labor relations: Development, structure, process.* 11th ed. New York, NY. McGraw-Hill Irwin.

Gerber, L. (2014). *The rise and decline of faculty governance; Professionalism and the modern American university.* Baltimore, MD. Johns Hopkins University Press.

Governance working group. (2012). Loyola Marymount University. Retrieved from http://www.lmu.edu/about/Faculty_Senate/Current_Issues/Governance/Governance_Working_Group.htm

Hansmann, H. (2012). Understanding education in the United States: The evolving economic structure of higher education. *University Of Chicago Law Review*, 79159.

Jaschik, S. (2012). Has faculty's role eroded? *Inside Higher Ed*. Retrieved from http://www.insidehighered.com/news/2012/07/09/college-associations-and-faculty-unions-argue-over-collective-bargaining-private.

Jones, W. A. (2012). Faculty involvement in institutional governance: A literature review. *Journal Of The Professoriate*, 6(1), 117-135.

Keller, G. (1983). *Academic strategy: The management revolution in American higher education*. Baltimore, MD. Johns Hopkins University Press.

Lambdin, P & Shapurji, D. (2011). The changing landscape of health benefit brokers compensation; Strategies for addressing the rising cost of broker compensation. Deloitte Consulting. Retrieved from http://www.deloitte.com/assets/Dcom-UnitedStates/Local%20Assets/Documents/us_lshc_BrokerCompensation_102011.pdf.

Metchick, R. H., & Singh, P. (2004). Yeshiva and faculty unionization in higher education. *Labor Studies Journal*, 28(4), 45-66.

National Labor Relations Board v. Yeshiva University, 444 U.S. 672 (1980). Retrieved from LexisNexis Academic database.

Ng, W. (2012). How one fortune 250 company used internal marketing to drive engagement. *Incentive Magazine*. Retrieved from http://www.incentivemag.com/Incentive-Programs/Engagement/Articles/How-One-Fortune-250-Company-Used-Internal-Marketing-to-Drive-Engagement/.

Point Park University (2012). National Labor Relations Board. Retrieved from http://www.nlrb.gov/case/06-RC-012276.

Ramo, K. (2001). The American Association of University Professors indicators of sound governance. Retrieved from http://www.aaup.org/NR/rdonlyres/88582027-8022-463A-9063-09073CD07766/0/indicatorsofsoundgovernance.pdf.

Riley, N. (2011). Why unions hurt higher education. *USA Today*. Retrieved from http://usatoday30.usatoday.com/news/opinion/forum/2011-03-03-column03_ST_N.htm

Thorton, S & Curtis, J. (2012). A very slow recovery; The annual report on the economic status of the profession 2011-2012. Retrieved from http://www.aaup.org/file/2011-12Economic-Status-Report.pdf.

Westcott, K. (2012). Brief of amicus curiae, American association of university professors, in support of petitioner, newspaper guild of Pittsburgh/communication workers of America local 38061, AFL0CIO, CLC. American Associate of University Professors. Retrieved from http://www.aaup.org/NR/rdonlyres/CFE2A35C-44AC-4F87-975D-E405CF5D5209/0/PointParkamicus.pdf.

White, M. (2013). Student loan debt crisis: How'd we get here and what happens next? *Time*. Retrieved from   http://business.time.com/2013/02/04/student-loan-debt-crisis-howd-we-get-here-and-what-happens-next/.

Table 1

Cost of Unionization

	Non-Union	Union	Total Differential
Faculty Salary	$ 7,803,700	$ 8,662,107	$ 901,327
Salary Driven Benefits	$ 390,185	$ 433,105	

Note: Faculty salaries represent 100 combined rank positions. Union rate is based on a 12 percent increase over the non-union rate. The salary-driven benefits represent retirement contribution based on a 5 percent employer contribution.

Table 2

Costs for Evaluation of Shared Governance Model

	Indirect			Direct			Total Costs
	Hours	Hourly Wage	Total	Hours	Hourly Fee	Total	
1. Initial Review by Administration							
Personnel							
Human Resources	40	$50	$ 2,000				
Senior Administrators	12	$98	$ 1,176				
Consultant							
Attorney				5	$ 300	$ 1,500	$ 4,676
2. Faculty Committee							
Personnel							
Faculty Committee	224	$ 48	$ 10,752				
Staff	32	$ 17	$ 544				
Senior Administrators	16	$ 89	$ 1,424				
Full Faculty	200	$ 48	$ 9,600				$ 22,320
3. Final Review & Implementation							
Personnel							
Human Resources	40	$ 50	$ 2,000				
Senior Administrators	12	$ 98	$ 1,176				
Consultant							
Attorney				5	$ 300	$ 1,500	$ 4,676
Total			$ 28,672			$ 3,000	$ 31,672

Note. The Human Resources wage rate based on average wage for the position in all institution types from the 2012-13 Administrative CUPA Salary Survey. The senior administrators are a mix of president, senior provost and two vice presidents from the same CUPA survey. Faculty rate is based on an average rate for Professor, Associate, and Assistant Professors for all institutions from the 2012-13 Faculty CUPA Salary Survey as well as the 2011-12 AAUP survey. The Attorney rate is based on the 2010-11 Attorney Rate Survey.

Table 3

Plan of Action Table

Step	Horizon	Parties & Resources
1. Initial Review		
• Review current governance • Review most recent implementation of faculty decisions/suggestions • Presentation of findings to President, Board, academic senior officers	Short term: 1-3 months	Resources reviewed by human resources & attorney: • Faculty Handbook • Faculty meeting minutes • Yeshiva doctrine mandates • Committee minutes – implementation of faculty originated policies and procedures
2. Governance Review Committee		

• Committee composition determination and installation
• Committee charge
• AAUP survey to determine current status
  o Curriculum, instruction & research;
  o Faculty status;
  o Student life issues related to education;
• Audits, recommendations, implementation & follow-up
	Long term:
	12-15 months
		Resources reviewed by committee:
		• Necessary internal & external stakeholders for establishing practice and communicating findings
		• Faculty committees (curriculum, personnel, faculty senate etc.)
		• AAUP governance guidance documents
		• Other institutional practices
		• Yeshiva doctrine documentation and analysis

3. Final Review		
• Audit of committee recommendations & updated procedures; • Return to committee of any findings needing clarity or missed in original recommendation; • Final review to President, Board, academic senior officers • Implementation and communication to broad stakeholders for successful compliance. • Ongoing/periodic review	Review: Short term: 2 months Maintenance: Long term: On-going	Resources reviewed by human resources & attorney: • Committee recommendations & associated documents; • Yeshiva doctrine mandates • Assignment of periodic review to a standing academic committee(s)

Tax Fraud:
The Journey from Civil Investigation to Criminal Prosecution and Back Again

Alisha M. Harper
Bellarmine University

ABSTRACT

The journey of a tax case from civil investigation to criminal prosecution is one that often confounds taxpayers and practitioners. Although criminal tax proceedings are possible with any case that has indicators of fraud, not all tax fraud results in criminal prosecution. This article will examine the rules surrounding both civil and criminal tax fraud under Title 26 by analyzing the progression of tax cases from civil inquiry to criminal action and the distinction between civil fraud and criminal penalties.

In addition, a recent law change affecting both civil and criminal tax cases will be considered. Internal Revenue Code § 6201(a)(4), enacted as part of the Firearms Excise Tax Improvement Act of 2010, P.L. 111-327, authorizes the IRS to assess and collect restitution in criminal tax cases as if it were a tax. The paper concludes with thoughts on the civil/criminal aspects of fraud, some suggestions for practitioners representing clients involving the potential for fraud, and some pitfalls of the new restitution assessment law that practitioners should be cognizant of.

Criminal Statutes

Title 26 criminal tax cases often begin the way any tax case begins, with the involvement of a civil Internal Revenue Service ("IRS") agent or officer. An IRS agent, representing the examination function of the IRS, will send a general letter explaining that the taxpayer is being audited. Alternatively, it may be an IRS officer, representing the collection function of the IRS, contacting the taxpayer concerning a tax balance due. Either of these seemingly mild events could result in a criminal tax investigation.

According to TRAC (Transactional Records Access Clearinghouse), during 2013, approximately 530 criminal prosecutions in the United States included a Title 26 criminal statute as the lead charge (TRAC, IRS Criminal Enforcement by District, Percent of Prosecutions with Tax Lead Charge). Of the 530 prosecutions, 430, or 81 percent, were either pursuant to Internal Revenue Code § 7201 or Internal Revenue Code § 7206.

Section 7201 is a felony statute that applies to "any person who willfully attempts in any manner to evade or defeat any tax imposed by this title or the payment thereof . . .." "Section 7201 proscribes the single crime of tax evasion, a crime which can be committed **either** by evading the assessment **or** the payment of taxes" (*U.S. v. Mal*). The first part of § 7201 (evade or defeat tax) is known as evasion of assessment and involves shielding taxable income to prevent the IRS from determining a taxpayer's tax liability; the second part of § 7201 (or payment thereof) is known as evasion of payment and involves placing assets outside of the reach of the IRS to prevent the collection of a taxpayer's tax liability (*Sansone v. U.S.*). Fraud comes into play when an IRS agent or officer suspects a taxpayer acted with the intent to evade assessment or collection.

7206 is a felony statute that applies to any person who, inter alia, "willfully makes and subscribes any return, statement, or other document, which contains or is verified by a written declaration that it is made under the penalties of perjury, and which he does not believe to be true and correct as to every material matter." Fraud comes into play when an IRS agent or officer suspects a taxpayer willfully submitted a false or fraudulent document.

Intent (for purposes of evasion or willfulness) is derived from objective factors the courts have branded "badges of fraud"; "circumstances so frequently attending fraudulent [transactions] that an inference of fraud arises from them" (*U.S. v. Leggett*). The most commonly identified badges of fraud include: "(1) understating income, (2) maintaining inadequate records, (3) giving implausible or inconsistent explanations of behavior, (4) concealing income or assets, (5) failing to cooperate with tax authorities, (6) engaging in illegal activities, (7) providing incomplete or misleading information to one's tax preparer, (8) giving testimony that lacks credibility, (9) filing false documents, including filing false income tax returns, (10) failing to file tax returns, and (11) dealing in cash" (*Laciny v. Commissioner*).

From Civil Investigation to Criminal Referral

Although there is only one evasion statute, the two elements of § 7201 follow different paths to result in charges of either evasion of assessment or evasion of payment. In assessment cases, the route generally begins with a civil examination.

In *U.S. v. Powell*, the IRS began an audit of Jesse Powell's 1978 tax return on or about October 23, 1980. During the first meeting with Mr. Powell, the IRS informed Mr. Powell that the audit was a civil examination. Early in the audit, the IRS agent noted large deposits into Mr. Powell's bank account from the "Executive IV Club." When questioned about the deposits, Mr. Powell denied that the deposits were rent or that he owned the building from which the club was operated. Subsequently, the IRS agent obtained copies of cancelled checks from the clubs' owner and an affidavit from the owner verifying that the deposits were, if fact, rent checks paid to Mr. Powell. When confronted with the checks and affidavit, Mr. Powell conceded the payments were rent, but stated the property and the money were for his children's trust; he simply failed to follow the legal requirements to form the trust. After further investigation, the IRS agent determined (using an indirect method of proving income) that Mr. Powell had spent substantially more money during the tax years under investigation than he reported on his tax return. The agent also discovered additional sources of unreported income. Mr. Powell subsequently changed his story concerning the account in which the rents were deposited claiming the account belonged to his father-in-law.

The *Powell* case illustrates several of the "badges of fraud" referenced including understating income, giving implausible or inconsistent explanations, concealing income and assets, and filing false documents, including his false income tax returns. On October 31, 1981, the IRS revenue agent referred the case to the IRS's criminal investigation division ("CID"). On April 27, 1982, Mr. Powell was informed he was under criminal investigation. Mr. Powell was convicted "on three counts of willfully attempting to evade federal income taxes," and sentenced to 2 years in prison and a $15,000 fine.

U.S. v. Threadgill is an example of the path from civil collection to criminal conviction. Mr. Threadgill's tax issues began when he filed his income tax return for 1985 reflecting a balance due of more than $150,000 which he failed to pay. Mr. Threadgill did eventually pay the balance due in June 1987; however, the IRS conducted an examination of Mr. Threadgill's 1985 tax return and determined he owed additional taxes. Throughout 1990 and into the 2000s, Mr. Threadgill's unpaid income tax liabilities grew. By 2004, Mr. Threadgill owed income tax to the U.S. government of more than $1,000,000. Throughout the 1990s and into 2000, the IRS followed the course for civil collection placing several liens on Mr. Threadgill's property and issuing numerous "Collection Due Process Notice of Intent to Levy" letters to Mr. Threadgill in an attempt to collect his unpaid income taxes. During this time frame, Mr. Threadgill submitted multiple "Offers in Compromise" to compromise his unpaid liabilities. These offers were all rejected by the IRS (except for 1 which Mr. Threadgill withdrew).

In 2005, the IRS began an investigation into Mr. Threadgill for "the purposeful evasion of payment of income taxes." The IRS attempted a field contact with Mr. Threadgill at his condominium (the "Water Place condo"). The IRS officer assigned the case left her card with contact information and notices advising Mr. Threadgill of his liability and rights as a taxpayer. Mr. Threadgill contacted the revenue officer and advised he was unable to pay the taxes. The IRS proceeded with its investigation of Mr. Threadgill and determined, from a financial analysis, that Mr. Threadgill had used his corporate bank account to pay a number of personal expenses; that Mr. Threadgill had transferred the Water Place condo into the name of a trust two days after contact by the IRS officer in 2005; and that Mr. Threadgill transferred assets into several bank accounts in the names of trusts (assets which he personally utilized). Mr. Threadgill's case was transferred to the CID for criminal investigation. Mr. Threadgill was found guilty of violating § 7201 and sentenced to 51 months imprisonment.

U.S. v. Peters and *U.S. v. Memmott* illustrate the path involving § 7206 convictions. *U.S. v. Peters* began in 1988, when Florence Peters former spouse contacted the IRS CID to report "improper tax reporting practices." An IRS CID agent met with Mr. Peters who provided numerous checks which he alleged represented personal expenses deducted by Mrs. Peters as business expenses on her tax returns. The CID agent determined that the information was an unsubstantiated allegation of fraud relating to expenses which may prove to be legitimate, and handed the file over to the IRS examination division. In March or April of 1990, the case was assigned to an IRS revenue agent who initiated a civil audit. On July 2, 1990, the IRS revenue agent sent a form letter to Florence Peters indicating that her 1987 and 1988 corporate tax returns had been selected for civil audit. The letter included a Privacy Act Notice and the standard Taxpayer Rights document. There was no indication the audit had been prompted by an informant or that the case had been referred by the CID.

The IRS revenue agent first met with Mrs. Peters in November 1990 to discuss a $100,000 discrepancy in her tax filings. Following this first meeting, the agent conducted several personal and telephone meetings with Mrs. Peters and her accountant, William Morrison. In April 1991, the agent concluded her audit and began to compose a fraud referral. She reviewed the case with her supervisor, who advised that the case was not developed to the point of a fraud referral and contained too many procedural errors (particularly certain disallowed expenses for which Mrs. Peters needed to be given the opportunity to explain). The case was reassigned to two revenue agents with no prior history with the case for a de novo review. In December 1991, the case was referred to the CID for a criminal investigation. Mrs. Peters was convicted of four counts of making false statements on her tax returns in violation of § 7206(1). The conviction related to Mrs. Peters filing returns claiming personal expenses as business deductions.

U.S. v. Memmott involves two separate criminal charges, I.R.C. § 7201 and I.R.C. § 7206. Both charges stem from collection action. In May 2005, following a Tax Court case involving Mr. Memmott's 1993 through 1996 income tax liabilities, Mr. Memmott's individual tax case was referred to an IRS revenue officer for civil collection action. The revenue officer had previously been involved in efforts to collect business taxes from a partnership Mr. Memmott had with his brother and son. During his workup of Mr. Memmott's individual tax case, and before meeting with Mr. Memmott, the revenue officer placed Mr. Memmott's case in "fraud development status." The revenue officer felt the case reflected "unanswered questions, possibly some suspicious activity." On June 9, 2005, Mr. Memmott met with the revenue officer to complete a Form 433-A, "Collection Information Statement for Wage Earners and Self-Employed Individuals," in his case. "Form 433-A is used to obtain current financial information necessary for determining how a wage earner or self-employed individual can satisfy an outstanding tax liability" (*U.S. v. Memmott*). Mr. Memmott signed the Form 433-A on June 9, 2005, under penalties of perjury. In April 2006, a special agent with the CID and the revenue officer met with Mr. Memmott to discuss perceived discrepancies on his Form 433-A.

It was determined that Mr. Memmott owned property that he failed to include on his Form 433-A. The facts showed that Mr. Memmott was the true owner of property which was titled to his mother (as nominee only). Mr. Memmott entered into the contract to purchase the property (showing only him as the purchaser); Mr. Memmott was involved in the lease of the property; the property was at one point titled to Mr. Memmott's ex-spouse and used to obtain loan proceeds which were transferred to Mr. Memmott for his personal use. Additionally, Mr. Memmott had obtained more than $700,000 from his investors in connection with his day trading activity which he used for his personal and business expenses. Although these funds were illegally obtained, "the existence of even illegal funds . . . must be disclosed in order to accurately determine the collectability of a taxpayer's debt" (*U.S. v. Memmott*). Mr. Memmott was convicted under § 7206(1) for filing a Form 433-A, signed under penalties of perjury, that he knew contained false information. Also relevant was Mr. Memmott's history as an attorney and experience in business and tax matters. Mr. Memmott was also convicted under § 7201 for evasion of payment.

Firm Indicators of Fraud

The cases discussed show the path from civil to criminal, but they also raise the question of when that step from civil to criminal should occur. When does an IRS revenue agent or revenue officer make a referral to the IRS Criminal Investigation Division?

Civil action is suspended when "firm indicators of fraud" or willfulness are established (IRM 25.1.3.2). The civil agent, with the assistance of a Fraud Technical Advisor, refers the case to the CID (IRM 25.1.3.1). This "firm indicators" determination is a factual one that is made on a case-by-case basis (*U.S. v. Peters*). The *Peters* case, discussed earlier, began with a tip from Florence Peters former spouse to the CID. Mrs. Peters filed a motion to suppress evidence in her criminal trial on the theory that the IRS obtained the evidence for her criminal prosecution "in violation of her Fourth and Fifth Amendment rights by telling her they were conducting a routine civil audit when in fact they were carrying out a criminal investigation" (*U.S. v. Peters*). This action to suppress evidence is also known as the "Tweel" defense named after the 5th Circuit case *U.S. v. Tweel*.

Nicholas J. Tweel, was convicted of conspiracy to defraud the United States, two counts of tax evasion under § 7201 and two counts of filing false documents under § 7206. He was sentenced to four years in prison and fined a total of $30,000. Tweel filed a motion to suppress evidence used in his criminal prosecution on the theory the evidence was improperly obtained.

The investigation leading up to Tweel's indictment began in May 1969, when a revenue agent with the IRS informed Tweel and his wife that their joint income tax returns for 1966 through 1968 were being audited. The letter requested that Tweel and his wife schedule an appointment to meet with the revenue agent. Tweel's accountant telephoned the revenue agent in June 1969 to postpone the appointment. The IRS had just completed an audit of Tweel's joint income tax returns for 1958 through 1963. The parties did schedule an appointment for August 1969.

As part of the audit for 1958 through 1963, a special agent of the CID became involved but eventually withdrew. The audit remained civil. In the course of the new audit (for 1966-1968), Tweel's accountant inquired whether a "special agent" was involved. The revenue agent replied in the negative, leading the accountant to believe this was a civil audit. What the revenue agent failed to mention is that the audit was being conducted at the specific request of the Organized Crime and Racketeering Section of the Department of Justice. The accountant presented the records he had with respect to Tweel's tax affairs and "also allegedly obtained additional records from Tweel to voluntarily present to [the revenue agent] for the new audit." Tweel's motion to suppress was based on the theory that the revenue agent's microfilming of Tweel's records "constituted an illegal search in violation of the Fourth Amendment because appellant's consent was obtained through deception."

A taxpayer's Fourth Amendment right is violated when an IRS revenue agent or officer proceeds with civil examination or collection action as a mask to obtain evidence for purposes of criminal prosecution (*U.S. v. Tweel*). Once "firm indicators of fraud" are present, civil action should cease and a criminal referral made so that the taxpayer can be made aware of his/her rights. A revenue agent or officer cannot outright lie about a potential criminal referral (IRM 25.1.3.2).

Although the failure to warn does not constitute fraud, deceit or trickery, silence can "be equated with fraud where there is a legal or moral duty to speak or where an inquiry left unanswered would be intentionally misleading" (*U.S. v. Prudden*). In *Tweel*, the revenue agent knew that the IRS was acting at the request of the Organized Crime and Racketeering Section; the revenue agent knew Tweel's accountant's inquiry about the involvement of a special agent was to determine whether his client was under criminal investigation; the revenue agent's response, although technically true, was misleading to such a degree that the consent (granted by providing Tweel's information for microfilming) was improperly obtained. The motion to suppress was granted.

Peters delves further into the question of "firm indicators of fraud." The *Peters* Court begins by noting that the revenue agents involved in Peter's examination characterized their investigation as a civil audit. The Court then goes on to determine that the facts do not support the conclusion that IRS had "firm indicators of fraud" prior to the criminal referral: that the examination resulted from an information item (contact by Peters' former spouse) was not a "firm indication of fraud;" the involvement of the CID in handing the case over to examination was not a "firm indication of fraud" in light of CID ceasing involvement in the examination case; continuing the examination after the initial revenue agent's determination to refer the case to CID was not a "firm indication of fraud;" the Court found that the audit continued because the initial agent's referral was defective and needed to be further developed.

Although the *Peters* Court relied on the "firm indications" rule, the Court explains the reservations it had in relying on this rule and notes two significant flaws in the rule. First, the rule lacks any definitive criteria. As explained by an IRS manager in the *Peters* case, "a firm indication of fraud is when I, as a group manager, sign the fraud referral form." Second, the rule implies that there is a "bifurcated system," a line between civil and criminal investigation that is only crossed when firm indicators are found. The problem with the bifurcation theory is that any "evidence gathered in a civil audit may be used in a criminal prosecution." In sum, the "firm indications" rule "invites the IRS to engage in "constructive dishonesty"" (*U.S. v. Peters*).

The *Peters* Court also addressed the "duty to warn." Internal Revenue Service agents and officers do not have a duty to disclose an audit may end in criminal investigation. Rather, the only circumstance in which the duty is imposed "is in response to a direct question from the taxpayer." This is in line with *Tweel*, wherein the accountant inquired about the involvement of a "special agent." It was this question that prompted the *Tweel* Court to rule in favor of the taxpayer. In addition, the IRS does not have a duty to advise a taxpayer that an audit was initiated based on an information item. Internal Revenue Code § 6103(i)(6) specifically prohibits such disclosure of information if it would identify a confidential informant.

The question presented and addressed by the U.S. District Court for the Eastern District of Michigan in *U.S. v. Rutherford* was a very specific one: when did the IRS have "firm indicators of fraud that should have terminated the civil investigation being conducted by the IRS." *Rutherford* concerned examination and collection activities involving a non-profit organization, Metro Emergency Services ("MES") and its president, Jon Rutherford. An IRS agent in the Tax Exempt and Government Entities Division ("TEGE") became involved in the case in May 2003 following an article that appeared in the Detroit Free Press in August 2001 concerning potential mismanagement of the nonprofit.

Following an initial review, the TEGE revenue agent contacted an IRS revenue officer, in July 2003, regarding unfiled Forms 941, used by employers to report employee Federal income tax withholding, and the collection of unpaid taxes. The July 2003 memorandum from the TEGE revenue agent to the IRS revenue officer specifically noted that the case was "filled with very large and significant indicators of fraud," but also noted that plausible explanations for the discrepancies could exist. A fraud technical advisor was also contacted in July 2003 to determine whether the case reflected first indicators of fraud. In August 2003, the TEGE agent along with his supervisor met with two fraud technical advisors to develop an action plan for the case including the involvement of a revenue agent to examine the individual tax returns of Jon Rutherford, a revenue agent to look at the possibility of excessive compensation, and a revenue officer to address the collection of unpaid taxes. In addition, the action plan included the collection of information from MES and third parties as well as an interview with Jon Rutherford. It was specifically noted that Mr. Rutherford reflected income tax withholding on his individual return that had never been remitted to the IRS. Following this August 2003 meeting, the fraud technical advisors felt there were "first indicators of fraud," but that further development would be necessary to make a conclusion on "firm indicators of fraud."

In October 2003, the IRS parties involved in the case held another meeting to discuss withholding taxes, transferred assets, unfiled tax returns, and officer compensation. Further action was proposed by one of the fraud technical advisors involved in the case to obtain the unfiled returns, file federal tax liens, identify properties, contact third parties, and interview Jon Rutherford as well as other parties involved at MES. Counsel for the IRS became involved in the case in November 2003. In December 2003, one of the IRS agents working the case met with Bernard Gibbons, the power of attorney for MES and Jon Rutherford, to obtain documents previously requested. At that time, Mr. Gibbons informed the IRS agent that Jon Rutherford was not willing to meet with IRS personnel. A follow-up meeting was scheduled for December 16, 2003.

Bernard Gibbons, Judith Bugaiski (the custodian of records for MES) and Jon Rutherford appeared at the December 16, 2003, meeting. The revenue agent collected additional documents and questioned Mr. Rutherford about a limited liability company formed by Mr. Rutherford in 1997 or 1998 to manage property, the unfiled Forms 941 and unpaid withholding taxes. Mr. Rutherford became agitated during the interview and informed the agent he wanted to leave. The agent advised Mr. Rutherford she needed additional information, but Mr. Rutherford terminated the interview.

In January 2004, two fraud technical advisors, two revenue officers, IRS counsel, a revenue agent, and a group manager held a lengthy meeting and discussed a potential criminal referral. According to all present, it was still too early to make the referral, i.e., there were not "firm indicators of fraud." A detailed list of further actions was set out following the January 2004 meeting including determining tax due and owing without requesting further return information, collection activities, and locating additional third parties to establish Rutherford's intent. Specifically noted in one of the memoranda was the need to determine whether the IRS had "firm indicators of fraud." On the same date as the civil meeting, the revenue agent, IRS counsel and group manager met with a special agent for the CID concerning whether a substitute return (prepared for the taxpayer by the IRS) would impact the criminal referral.

Following this January 2004 meeting, the revenue agent continued to try to meet with Jon Rutherford and Judith Bugaiski. After several failed attempts, she issued separate summonses to Rutherford and Bugaiski as members of DPR, the limited liability company Rutherford had formed. In June 2004, Mr. Rutherford and Ms. Bugaiski were interviewed on four separate occasions by two different IRS revenue agents concerning MES and DPR.

On July 20, 2004, the IRS civil division decided to make three criminal referrals, one for DPR Management, LLC one for Jon Rutherford, and one for Judith Bugaiski. Jon Rutherford and Judith Bugaiski were charged with multiple counts of income tax evasion for failure to pay pursuant to § 7201, willful failure to pay over tax pursuant to § 7202, false or fraudulent statements pursuant to § 7206, and conspiracy pursuant to 18 U.S.C. § 371.

The Michigan District Court, following *Peters*, initially notes that the determination of firm indicators of fraud "is not an easy one. It must be determined on a case by case basis from the totality of the facts" (*U.S. v. Rutherford*). The Court goes on to enunciate certain principles applicable to this concept of "firm indicators." First, the Court, quoting *U.S. v. McKee*, explains that an IRS agent or officer who continues to conduct a civil audit or proceed with civil collection action after firm indicators have been developed "is, in fact, making affirmative misrepresentations to the constitutional detriment of the taxpayer." Second, the Court points out that a taxpayer should be given an opportunity to explain after "first indicators" are determined. Finally, the Court states that "the agent and his supervisor should enjoy great latitude and deference."

After asserting these general principles, the Court concluded that the IRS had firm indicators prior to the issuance of the summonses and subsequent interviews in June 2004. Specifically, the Court observed that the IRS knew numerous tax returns were unfiled in June 2003 and that Mr. Rutherford's explanation was unsatisfactory; that an IRS agent drafted a memorandum in July 2003 noting "very large and significant indicators of fraud;" that the fraud technical advisor noted a withholding tax discrepancy in August 2003 with respect to Mr. Rutherford's individual tax returns; Rutherford's agitation during and termination of his interview in December 2003; and the lengthy January 2004 meeting between several functions of the IRS about the criminal referral of this case. In the end, the Court found that the "first indicators of fraud morphed into firm indicators" once Mr. Rutherford and Ms. Bugaiski were given the opportunity to explain discrepancies during the first interview in December 2003 and "chose to truncate their explanations and Mr. Rutherford stomped out."

The United States appealed the *Rutherford* case to the Sixth Circuit Court of Appeals which Court overruled the District Court and concluded that there were no due process violations requiring suppression of evidence. Reviewing the facts presented to the District Court, the Sixth Circuit conceded that the IRS agents and officers involved in the Rutherford/MES case may have acted in a manner contrary to the IRS's Internal Revenue Manual in failing to make a referral to the CID when "firm indicators" were present; however, the Court found that such actions did not violate the Due Process Clause as "there was no deception or trickery" by the civil agents involved in the case (*U.S. v. Rutherford* 6th Cir.).

The concept of "firm indicators of fraud" is an indefinable one. The cases that address this issue all include language similar to that found in the cases analyzed here, "it must be determined on a case by case basis from the totality of the facts." The best answer to the question of when the IRS has "firm indicators" is found in the words of the IRS manager in the *Peters* case, "a firm indication of fraud is when I, as a group manager, sign the fraud referral form." Even more problematic is the Sixth Circuit's reversal of the District Court's opinion in *Rutherford*. This reversal and the conclusions of the Sixth Circuit make clear that the real question is one of deceit or trickery. When firm indicators are determined is irrelevant; a due process violation only occurs with deceit or trickery on the part of the IRS agents and officers.

Criminal Prosecution

In recent years, the CID has accepted less than 70 percent of fraud referrals (Treasury Inspector General Tax Administration ("TIGTA") Fraud Referral Report p. 3)1. The CID, however, does not have the final say on criminal tax prosecution. The Department of Justice Tax Division is responsible for supervising the criminal tax enforcement program which includes criminal proceedings relating to the internal revenue laws (28 C.R.F. § 0.70; DOJ Tax Division Criminal Tax Manual § 1.01[4][a]). Nevertheless, the numbers show that around 90 percent of all prosecutions recommended by the CID are accepted by the Department of Justice ("DOJ") and U.S. Attorney's Office (TIGTA Fraud Referral Report p.3).

Once the case is accepted by the CID, the DOJ, and the U.S. Attorney's Office, an information/indictment is filed against the taxpayer/defendant. According to the Sourcebook of Criminal Justice Statistics, approximately 95 percent of criminal tax cases result in conviction and sentencing. Of this 95 percent, approximately 90 percent are resolved by plea agreement2.

Incarceration and Restitution

A judge can order restitution for Title 26 tax offenses **only** if the parties agree; thus, a plea agreement may include restitution, incarceration, or both as part of the sentencing (18 U.S.C. §§ 3663(a)(3) & 3563(b)(2); *Batson*, 608 F.3d 630 (9th Cir. 2010); *Townsend on Federal Tax Crimes*). The incarceration rate for fraud referral convictions for the fiscal years 2011 and 2012 ranged from 81-83 percent (TIGTA Fraud Referral Report p. 4). Convicted taxpayers generally served, or are serving, between 24 and 28 months in a federal prison (TIGTA Fraud Referral Report p. 4).

Effective in 2010, Internal Revenue Code § 6201(a)(4) authorizes the Secretary to "assess and collect the amount of restitution under an order pursuant to § 3556 of title 18, United States Code, for failure to pay any tax imposed under this title (Title 26) in the same manner as if such amount were such tax." Internal Revenue Code § 6201(a)(4) further provides that the underlying

---

1 In a report published by TIGTA on May 24, 2013, the CID's fraud referral acceptance rate for 2011 and 2012 was 68.3% and 66.7%, respectively.
2 This information is garnered from a review of online statistics for the fiscal years 2002 through 2010.

tax liability assessed pursuant to a restitution order cannot be challenged. Additionally, such assessment may be made at any time. 26 U.S.C. § 6501(c)(11). Internal Revenue Code § 6213 was also amended to make clear that a notice of assessment of restitution is not a notice of deficiency giving the taxpayer rights to petition the Tax Court; is not a notice of deficiency restricting the issuance of further deficiency letters; and is not a notice of deficiency prohibiting any credits or refunds after a petition to the Tax Court. 26 U.S.C. § 6213(b)(5).

The law is clear that the assessment is permitted for "failure to pay" any Title 26 taxes. The restitution order must be traceable to a tax imposed by Title 26 (CC Notice 2011-018). The assessment should include any interest on the underpayment pursuant to I.R.C. § 6601 determined at the underpayment rate established by I.R.C. § 6621. However, the restitution assessment cannot include any penalties or additional tax determined by the examination division (CC Notice 2011-018). If the IRS's civil division wishes to assess penalties and/or additional tax, it must conduct a full examination and issue a notice of deficiency. The collection rights ensured by I.R.C. §§ 6320 and 6330 (collection due process) apply to collection of the assessed restitution amounts (CC Notice 2011-018). However, the taxpayer is precluded from contesting the underlying liability based on restitution (I.R.C. § 6201(a)(4)(C)).

The Road Back: Civil Fraud

In all cases where fraud is considered, even if the case is not accepted by CID for prosecution, an examining agent must document why the civil fraud penalty is not asserted (IRM 25.1.5.2(4)). When criminal prosecution has been recommended by the criminal division to the Department of Justice, a civil examination agent can only remove fraud penalties (civil fraud or fraudulent failure to file) with concurrence from the IRS Office of Chief Counsel (IRM 25.1.6.2(5)).

Internal Revenue Code § 6663 imposes a penalty of 75 percent on any underpayment of tax attributable to fraud. Internal Revenue Code § 6651(f) increases the failure to file penalty from a maximum penalty of 25 percent to a maximum penalty of 75 percent if the failure to file a return is fraudulent. These civil penalties can be imposed on any taxpayer, but the assertion of the penalties is practically guaranteed for a taxpayer with a Title 26 (tax) criminal conviction.

The same badges of fraud utilized in criminal Title 26 convictions are also employed in civil fraud cases. "Courts have developed a nonexclusive list of factors or 'badges of fraud' that demonstrate fraudulent intent. These badges of fraud include: (1) Understatement of income; (2) inadequate records; (3) implausible or inconsistent explanations of behavior; (4) concealment of income or assets; (5) failure to cooperate with tax authorities; (6) filing false documents; (7) failure to make estimated tax payments; (8) dealing in cash; (9) engaging in illegal activities; and (10) engaging in a pattern of behavior that indicates an intent to mislead" (*Prater v. Commissioner*). The largest distinction between civil and criminal fraud cases lies in the standard of proof. In criminal cases, the United States must prove fraud beyond a reasonable doubt. The standard in the civil arena is clear and convincing evidence (*Carlson v. U.S.*).

To this end, if the taxpayer is convicted pursuant to I.R.C. § 7201, the evasion statute, the IRS can rely on collateral estoppel to prevent the taxpayer from disputing he or she acted with the intent to evade or defeat taxes necessary for the civil fraud penalty to apply (26 U.S.C. §§ 6663 or 6651(f)) on the rationale that the requisite intent to evade or defeat tax was established during the criminal case (*Amos v. Commissioner*). If, however, the Title 26 conviction is a statute other than § 7201, as most are3, or, the IRS wants to pursue civil fraud following an acquittal of the taxpayer, rejection by CID, or without a CID referral, the IRS must conduct a full fraud examination.

As an example, Anthony and Shirley Olbres were indicted for 3 counts of income tax evasion pursuant to I.R.C. § 7201 for the tax year 1986, 1987, and 1988 (*U.S. v. Olbres*). Mr. and Mrs. Olbres were convicted of evasion for the 1987 tax year; but, acquitted for the 1986 and 1988 tax years. Following the conclusion of the Olbres' criminal case, the IRS pursued civil fraud penalties pursuant to I.R.C. § 6653 (currently § 6663). The United States Tax Court heard the civil matter and concluded that taxpayers' were "estopped from denying fraud for 1987 because of their conviction for criminal tax evasion under § 7201 for that year" (*Olbres v. Commissioner*). In addition, the Tax Court concluded that the IRS had met its burden of proving **by clear and convincing** evidence that taxpayers' intended to evade tax for the 1986 and 1988 tax years and upheld the IRS's assertion of the civil fraud penalties for 1986 and 1988 as well.

The Last Stop: Suggestions and Pitfalls

Criminal tax cases often begin with civil action (a civil audit or collection). Practitioners should be aware that there is no clear line of transition from civil to criminal. As the case law notes, the question of firm indicators of fraud is one of judgment on the part of the IRS. If a practitioner suspects that fraud is an issue, the only way to be sure is to ask the question. The taxpayer's constitutional protections prevent the IRS from collecting information for a criminal prosecution while maintaining that the case is merely a civil examination. However, these protections come into play only if there is blatant deceit or misrepresentation, i.e., only if the question is asked and answered.

Working with the restitution law presents several potential pitfalls for tax practitioners. First is calculation of tax loss. Restitution is assessable "as if" it were a tax (I.R.C. § 6201(a)(4)). Dealing with the tax loss up front allows practitioners to be mindful of the amount of restitution agreed to and the implications surrounding assessment and collection of restitution to avoid the IRS collecting more tax than is actually due. Of important note is language in § 2T1.1(c) of the Federal Sentencing Guidelines Manual providing that percentages apply in calculating tax loss. For example, "[i]f the offense involved filing a tax return in which gross income was underreported, the tax loss shall be treated as equal to 28% of the unreported gross income (34% if the taxpayer is a corporation) plus 100% of any false credits claimed against tax." Or, "[i]f the offense involved failure to file a tax return, the tax loss shall be treated as equal to 20% of the gross income (25% if the taxpayer is a corporation) less any tax withheld or otherwise paid, unless a more accurate determination of the tax loss can be made." These calculations and percentages do not take into account any additional deductions the taxpayer may be entitled to and certainly do not equate to the definition of a "deficiency" provided in the Internal Revenue Code. Further, the "tax loss" number presented by the government is utilized by the court to

---

3 For the fiscal year 2011, more than 1,100 tax crimes were successfully prosecuted. The lead charge in 183 of those cases was I.R.C. § 7201, while I.R.C. § 7206 was the lead charge in 238 cases (TRAC, IRS Criminal Enforcement by District, Percent of Prosecutions with Tax Lead Charge).

determine the sentence imposed on the taxpayer/defendant (United States Sentencing Commission (2011)). Rather than waiting until the sentencing to address this number, it would be better to address the number at the outset of the case and reduce the potential sentence for your client.

Additionally, the IRS's position that the restitution amount is an "as if" tax means that the IRS is not allowing any offsets for the restitution order. In *CCN 2013-012*, the IRS makes its position clear by specifically stating that although Net Operating Loss "carrybacks, carryovers and other deductions" can be applied to reduce a taxpayer's civil liability, the IRS is required to collect the full amount of restitution ordered. The end result is that the IRS will collect more tax than is due if the restitution amount does not properly reflect the civil tax liability.

Second, practitioners should consider including penalties in the restitution order. Pursuant to the Internal Revenue Manual, the IRS civil division is required to consider civil fraud penalties in any case referred to the criminal division. If the criminal case results in prosecution, the civil division must assert civil fraud penalties (unless IRS Counsel determines that pursuance is not appropriate). If the conviction (by jury or plea) is pursuant to I.R.C. § 7201, evasion, collateral estoppel applies to any civil action and civil fraud penalties will apply. By including the penalties in the restitution agreement, the practitioner may save the client the burden and hassle of proceeding with subsequent civil action.

If, however, the conviction is pursuant to any other provision, the practitioner should examine how the government obtained the information for conviction. A grand jury investigation is generally instigated if the administrative process is insufficient to timely obtain the necessary information or "the investigation has proceeded as far as the administrative process allows," and a grand jury would strengthen prosecution potential (IRM 9.5.2.2). At the conclusion of a grand jury case that resulted in a final adjudication (conviction or plea), a closing letter is prepared that includes language terminating the criminal referral and seeking civil action (IRM 9.5.14.3). Federal Rule of Criminal Procedure 6(e) prevents disclosure of information obtained during a grand jury proceeding. Thus, in conducting its examination to determine the taxpayer/defendant's tax deficiency and establish the requisite intent for successful assertion of the civil fraud penalties, the civil division of the IRS is not entitled to the information gathered by the criminal division during the grand jury investigation.

If the information is obtained via a grand jury, and such information would not otherwise be available to the civil division of the IRS, the taxpayer may be better served by allowing the IRS to attempt to pursue the civil penalties after the criminal prosecution. In a report published by TIGTA, TIGTA reviewed a sample of 90 restitution payments made by 62 persons convicted of tax crimes. The review revealed that less than 1/3 of criminal tax cases involving restitution resulted in assessment of a civil tax against the taxpayer/defendant and application of restitution payments to the proper account before the enactment of I.R.C. § 6201(a)(4) authorizing assessment and collection of criminal restitution (*TIGTA Final Audit Report* (p. 5)).

Finally, practitioners should be mindful of joint accounts and conspiracy cases. With respect to joint return cases where only one spouse is indicted and enters into a plea that includes assessable restitution, if the assessment is not on a joint account, it is reasonable to believe the

IRS will issue a notice of deficiency to the other spouse. Tax practitioners must take care that the IRS does not then collect the "tax" from both the restitution amount agreed to by the indicted spouse and the deficiency, if any, subsequently assessed against the unindicted spouse. Further, if both spouses from a joint return are indicted and enter into a plea that includes assessable restitution, tax practitioners will have to address the issue of calculating "tax loss," the proper allocation of restitution, and/or the collection of restitution in order to avoid the IRS assessing and collecting more tax than is due.

Even greater questions arise with conspiracy cases. The new law raises serious concerns about assessing restitution as a tax and then proceeding to collect against a co-conspirator who is not the "taxpayer". As noted in *CCN 2013-012*, "[t]he distinction between criminal restitution and tax liability is perhaps most starkly presented when a return preparer . . . is ordered to pay restitution calculated with reference to the tax owed by his clients, a tax for which the return preparer is not civilly liable." Tax practitioners and the government will have to account for assessable restitution among co-conspirators to avoid the IRS assessing and collecting more tax than is due.

Conclusion

The path from civil administrative action to criminal prosecution and back is a rocky road for taxpayers and practitioners. There is no clear point when the line crosses from first indicators of fraud to firm indicators of fraud. Practitioners should be weary when cases present with any of the "badges of fraud."

Additionally, the new restitution assessment authority raises issues for tax practitioners to consider concerning plea agreements and tax collection. Tax practitioners need to consider whether the restitution amount represents the correct tax due keeping in mind that, once agreed to, the amount cannot be disputed without going back to the district court to amend the order. Also, for those practitioners representing noncriminal spouses or co-conspirators, the correct tax due and owing should only be collected once. If there are multiple assessments of the same amount, the practitioner needs to ensure the "liability" has not already been paid in full.

References

2011 Federal Sentencing Guidelines Manual.

University at Albany, Hindelang Criminal Justice Research Center, *Sourcebook of Criminal Justice Statistics*. Table 5.34.2002-2010. (*http://www.albany.edu/sourcebook/pdf/t5342010.pdf*) [*Oct. 26, 2014*].

Amos v. Commissioner, 43 T.C. 50 (1964).

Begg, M.E., Jones, F.W., Kisler, B., Hynes, D.J., Tengesdal, D.M., Chriest, T.A., Chiappino, J.J., Filippeli, M.F., Green, G.M., Hillenbrand, M.J., Jones, J.K., Zuika, J (2012). Procedures are Needed to Improve the Accounting and Monitoring of Restitution Payments to Prevent Erroneous

Refunds. TIGTA Report Reference No. 2012-30-012.

Begg, M.E., Cook, A.R., Aley, C., Dunleavy, F., Jones, F., Kisler, B., Hynes, D., Green, G., Anderson, T., & O'Connor, F. (2013). Actions Are Needed to Accurately Reflect Criminal Investigation's Fraud Referral Evaluation Period and Improve the Criminal Fraud Referral Process. TIGTA Report Reference No. 2013-30-051.

Carlson v. U.S., 113 AFTR 2d 2014-2542 (11th Cir. 2014).

Chief Counsel Notice 2011-018, www.irs.gov/pub.irs-ccdm/cc-2011-018.pdf

Chief Counsel Notice 2013-012, www.irs.gov/pub/irs-ccdm/cc_2013_012.pdf

Department of Justice Tax Division Criminal Tax Manual 1.01[4][a].

Internal Revenue Manual (IRM)

Laciny v. Commissioner, T.C. Memo. 2013-107, citing *Spies v. United States*, 317 U.S. 492, 499 (1943); *Conti v. Commissioner*, 39 F.3d *Commissioner*, 899 F.2d 164, 168 (2d Cir. 1990); *Scallen v. Commissioner*, 877 F.2d 1364, 1370 (8th Cir. 1989), aff'g T.C. Memo. 1987-412; *Bradford v. Commissioner*, 796 F.2d at 307-308; *Recklitis v. Commissioner*, 91 T.C. 874, 910 (1988).

Olbres v. Commissioner, T.C. Memo. 1997-437.

Prater v. Commissioner, T.C. Memo. 2011-100.

Sansone v. U.S., 381 U.S. 343 (1965).

Townsend, Jack (2012). *Townsend on Federal Tax Crimes* 2011 ed. 01, Revisions through 01/20/2012.

Transactional Records Access Clearinghouse (TRAC), IRS Criminal Enforcement by Distribution, Percent of Prosecutions with Tax Lead Charge, http://trac.syr.edu/phptools/enforcement/irsfree.php.

U.S. v. Batson, 608 F.3d 630 (9th Cir. 2010).

U.S. v. Leggett, 292 F.2d 423, 427 (6th Cir. 1961).

U.S. v. Mal, 942 F.2d 682, 686 (9th Cir. 1991).

U.S. v. McKee, 192 F.3d 535, 542 n5 (6th Cir. 1999).

U.S. v. Memmott, 112 AFTR 2d 2013-5864 (E.D. CA 2013).

U.S. v. Olbres, 99 F.3d 1129 (NH Dist. Ct. 1994).

U.S. v. Peters, 81 AFTR2d 98-737 (N.D. IL 1996), aff'd 153 F.3d 445 (7th Cir. 1998).

U.S. v. Powell, 835 F.2d 1095 (5th Cirt. 1988).

U.S. v. Prudden, 424 F.2d 1021 (5th Cir. 1970).

U.S. v. Rutherford, 99 AFTR 2d 2007-3223 (E.D. MI 2007).

U.S. v. Rutherford, 103 AFTR 2d 2009-702 (6th Cir. 2009).

U.S. v. Threadgill, 114 AFTR 2d 2014-5184 (6th Cir. 2014).

U.S. v. Tweel, 550 F. 2d 297 (5th Cir. 1977).

Psychological Disconnect: The Impact of Managerial Narrative on Perceptions of the Cessation of the Employee-Employer Relationship

Sean Walker
University of Tennessee at Martin

ABSTRACT

Recently, research has begun to focus on the impact of how words used by organizational members can impact perceptions and behaviors of employees and management during organizational events. The current research consisted of two studies that analyzed how managerial narrative, specifically the utilization of inclusive versus exclusive terminology, influenced a range of organizational perceptions following the termination of the employee/employer relationship. Study 1 found that managerial narrative impacted the individuals anger level, willingness to speak out negatively about the organization, willingness to take behavioral action (sue, file a complaint), their desire to seek more information, and the extent in which they felt they were treated with respect and empathy. Study 2 found, counter to predictions and prior research, that the directional influence of managerial narrative on perceptions of downsizing was the opposite of what was predicted. Coupled with previous research, the current findings contribute to the proposal of a new theoretical way of thinking about how to influence perceptions in the workplace, psychological distancing. Implications and future directions are discussed.

Introduction

Organizational behavior scholars commonly link psychological phenomena with organizationally and managerial relevant constructs. This interdisciplinary approach allows for a broader utilization of theoretical foundations to explain why and how organizational members may behave. Because it is of great importance for organizations to operate in as efficient manner as possible, much of the recent research in organizational behavior has focused or addressed how this can be done. More recent research has, and needs to continue to be, focused on how organizations can improve their performance by reducing the number of resources they input to derive the same amount of outputs or by increasing the amount of outputs with the given inputs. In the context of the current study it is the focus on the former, as opposed to the latter, that is most meaningful. In other words, how can organizations continue to improve (i.e. become more efficient) by putting forth fewer organizational resources (i.e. inputs). The current study seeks to provide one such assertion for achieving such an increase in efficiency by utilizing possibly the cheapest organizational resource, managerial narrative. Specifically, how can the inclusivity versus exclusivity of terminology influence perceptions of the cessation of the employment relationship (as measured by termination interviews and downsizing)? As such, the current research proposes that the way in which a manager talks to a terminated employee, whether terminated individually (in a termination interview) or collectively (downsizing victim) will have a significant impact on their perceptions of how the employment relationship was terminated. This is particularly important because it illustrates a new avenue of research for understanding the profound impact of words (i.e. which helps the organization become more efficient) and to managerial practice as it provides a new way for management to control the perception of the organization by an important stakeholder in the company (i.e. terminated employees). As such, the current study seeks to elucidate this linkage by utilizing two scenario based studies assessing the impact of managerial narrative on perceptions of termination interviews (study 1) and downsizing (study 2).

Literature Review

While there is some research focusing on the process of conducting termination interviews, there are still a myriad of black box issues that need to be elucidated. To date, prior work focuses mainly on effects of downsizing on layoff victims and survivors (Armstrong-Stassen, 2002; Brockner, 1988, 1994; Brockner Davy, & Carter, 1985; Brockner, Grover, O'Malley, Reed, & Glynn, 1993; Brockner Grover, Reed, Dewitt, & O'Malley, 1987; Leana & Feldman, 1988, 1990; O'Neill & Lenn, 1995; Pugh, Skarlicki, & Passell, 2003; Shah, 2000), workplace violence (e.g. Nigro and Waugh, 1996), effects of mergers and acquisitions (Schwieger and Ivancevich, 1987), and legal aspects (Sidebotham, 2005). Most of the research in this area comes from the downsizing literature which focuses primarily on the psychological and physiological variables that impact organizationally relevant members (i.e. survivors, management, victims) and measures psychological variables such as self-esteem (e.g. Kates, Greiff, and Hagen, 1990), well-being (Hepworth, 1980), and ethical implications (e.g. Miller, 2001), along with studies looking at the impact of downsizing on physical well-being (e.g. Cobb and Kasl, 1977). Within this stream of literature, research has focused on perceptions of organizationally relevant members but has neglected other important contextual factors that may impact how management should conduct the termination interview. In fact, Schwieger and Ivancevich (1987, p.128) explored the impact of terminations following corporate acquisition and found that "it was apparently not the terminations per se that created bitterness, but the manner in which the terminations were handled." Greenberg (1990) found that layoff survivors demonstrated higher levels of organizational commitment when they perceived that termination victims had been treated equitably. Gilliland and Schepers (2003) found that the manner in which managers' treated layoff victims was contingent upon the managers' perception of the employee's contribution to the success of the organization. In other words, this suggests that it is the context (the how) the termination is conducted that may be the primary predictor of the reaction by those involved in terminations/downsizing.

Despite all that is known about downsizing, little research has directly examined how termination interviews should be conducted based on the impact it may have on the terminated employee's reactions. There is currently a growing body of research attempting to fill-in the blanks with regard to employee reactions (e.g. Sidebotham, 2005; Wood & Karau, 2008; Zinn, 1988). This stream of research suggests managers narrative remaining positive (i.e. mentioning strong points of the terminated employee), allowing them to collect their belongings unescorted (e.g. Bayer, 2000), the necessity of a third party being present (e.g. Jesseph, 1989); and management reducing legal culpability of the company (e.g. Quinley, 2003). Similarly, Wood and Karau (2008) examined participant's reactions to how a hypothetical termination interview was conducted. They found that mentioning positives produced less anger, decreased one's likelihood to complain about the organization, decreased the likelihood the individual would seek legal action against the company, while increasing the perception that the termination was conducted fairly and that the manager demonstrated empathy.

The importance for handling such issues with a degree of tact and decorum circles around the idea that an employee that is terminated, who believes they were treated fairly by the organization, may serve as a source of positive advertising for the organization. Put differently, the fair and proper treatment of an ex-employee provides a rich repository of information for how current and future employees may be treated. Popular press discussions have also assessed this issue and seem to focus around the need for management to avoid certain types of statements (e.g. Quinley, 2003; Segal, 2009) and make sure to make others. For example, it would likely be well-received by the individual if management utilized a statement that thanked them for their contributions during their tenure with the organization.

All of this research illustrates the need to continue assessing other contextual factors that impact perceptions of termination interviews. In accordance with the current study, it is important to focus on the managerial narrative used during the termination interview. Because the current research focuses on two levels or perspectives of the cessation of the employment relationship (termination of the individual done individually and termination of the individual when done collectively), the next section focuses on pertinent work in the downsizing literature that may impact perceptions of how the termination was conducted.

Downsizing Literature

Downsizing is a prevalently studied and diverse literature. Scholars typically focus on the physical or psychological reactions downsizing can foster on a myriad of organizational members (e.g. survivors, management, and victims of downsizing). A fairly recent stream of literature has focused on the financial ramifications of downsizing. Specifically, much of this research has taken a longitudinal approach to analyze the finances of the firm before and after downsizing (e.g. Cascio, 1998) in an attempt to assess downsizing's prevalence on the organization. Important for the current study, which is focusing on attitudes or reactions to downsizing, the results have been mixed as some of the research finds positive results (e.g. Bruton & Keels, 1996; Cascio, 1993; Wayhan & Werner, 2000) whereas other studies have generated negative financial results (e.g. De Meuse, Vanderheiden, & Bergmann, 1994; Fisher & White, 2000) while others have shown that the financial results are virtually unchanged (e.g. Cascio, Young, & Morris, 1997).

In a body of literature that runs parallel with the current study, studies assessing the impact of downsizing on survivors (e.g. Brockner, 1988, 1994; Brockner, Grover, Reed, Dewitt, & O'Malley, 1987) typically focuses on the cognitive responses/evaluations (e.g. Cobb, Wooten, & Folger, 1995) and/or perceptions of procedural justice (e.g. Brockner, 1994, 2002, 2006).

A second stream of literature of interest to the current studies focus on perceptions of downsizing assesses the impact of such events on those individuals charged with terminating employees (i.e. the manager announcing or making the downsizing decision). Research has assessed a myriad of physiological and psychological reactions the layoff or terminating agent as they are commonly called (e.g. Grunberg, Moore, & Greenberg 2006; Noronha & D'Cruz, 2005) including variables that exacerbate these issues for the terminating/layoff agent (e.g. Brockner et al., 1987; Clair, Dufresne, Jackson, & Ladge, 2006; Noronha & D'Cruz, 2005, 2006) and coping mechanisms utilized by the layoff agent (e.g. Clair et al., 2006; Folger & Skarlicki, 1998; Grunberg et al., 2006).

Many organizational theorists focus on the behavioral, physiological, and psychological impact of the employees that are victims of downsizing. This stream of research assesses a wide range of variables from perceptions of procedural justice following the downsizing (e.g. Bies, Martin, & Brockner, 1993), coping strategies (e.g. Bennett, Martin, Bies, & Brockner, 1995; Kinicki, Prussia, & McKee-Ryan, 2000), and financial difficulties and organizational commitment issues (e.g. Leana & Feldman, 1992).

Theoretical Analysis & Hypotheses Development

While there is currently no clear theoretical foundation in which to proceed when studying perceptions of the cessation of the employee-employer relationship, there are some perspectives that we can glean insight on how narrative may impact these perceptions. Specifically, the current discussion will focus on the congruence and consistency of the behavioral and perceptual reactions of the individual being terminated (i.e. whether individually in a termination interview or as a collective as in downsizing initiatives) has on important and related psychological phenomenon such as respect, empathy, and perceptions of authenticity or genuineness of the proceeding.

Terminations, whether done individually or collectively, are major events in the organizational life and need to be treated with a degree of tact and care to safeguard against adverse psychological reactions. Terminology that is inconsistent, i.e. not typically used by the organization, or incongruent with the situation, i.e. doesn't fit the context, may impact the perceived harshness of the situation. This perspective is consistent with the prevalently used contingency theory originally derived by Woodward (1958) and later amended by Fiedler (1964). This theory states that the prescribed method for handling each situation is contingent on the variables present at that time and as such will fluctuate or need to be amended on a case-by-case basis. In other words, how you talk to one employee may not work well with another. Furthermore, a more direct approach or leadership style may work for some subordinates but not for others. In the context of the cessation of the employment relationship, when breaking bad news to an employee, it is likely that the terminology used to "break" this news to some employees will need to be changed/amended to fit the requirement of that individual. Some employees may view the terminology as being condescending or having a lack of respect for themselves. Furthermore, some employees may be more or less well received to hearing certain types of terminology.

One of the important perceptions an individual has during any social interaction is that they are being treated with respect. The concept of being treated with respect dates back to Immanuel Kant's (1785) seminal work in which Kant stated "act so that you will treat humanity, whether in your own person or in that of another, always as an end and never as a means only" (p. 420). In other words, treating a human being as an object (or as a means to an end) would be a violation of being treated with respect (Boatright, 2003) and also posited by Wood and Karau (2008). Wood and Karau (2008) argued that this level of respect does not end with the end of the employment relationship but must also be conducted during the cessation of the relationship (i.e. during termination).

One factor that may impact perceptions of whether or not management needs to tailor its utilization of different terminology with individuals, (i.e. treating them with respect) revolves around the inclusion of empathy. Empathy is the consideration of one's feelings in the process of making intelligent decisions (Goleman, 1998). A manager that can emphasize their level of empathy for the terminated individual(s) may be able to decrease the severity of the situation thus decreasing(increasing) the negative(positive) perceptions of the termination. This logic seems to be supported by Vallero and Vesilind (2006) who posited that engineers must incorporate empathy in an effort to prevent disputes. Goleman (1998) asserted that effective management requires the individual to utilize an empathetic viewpoint while considering others' emotions. In other words, the consideration of an employees' emotions during the termination will likely influence the employees perception of how the termination was conducted/handled. Put differently, if an individual feels as if they were treated unjustly (Scher & Heise, 1993), it is likely that the individual will perceive the termination more negatively.

There is an established stream of literature that acknowledges the influence of managerial language during organizational events. Scholars (e.g. Fiol, 2002; Giola & Chittipeddi, 1991) have found that managers may use narrative or symbols amend the currently used organizational meaning systems by unfreezing the current way of thinking, establishing new meanings, and refreezing the new belief system. This process of unfreezing, shifting of meaning systems, and refreezing comes from Lewin (1951) seminal work on the management of change. The concept of shifting meanings has been supported by the utilization of managerial narrative (e.g. Barry & Elmes, 1997; Brown, 1998) and typically focuses on the creation of meaning systems that are distinct from other organizational stories. The utilization of managerial narrative allows for the capturing of how these events are related to one another over time (Gergen & Gergen, 1997) in specific contexts (Gergen, Gergen, & Barrett, 2004) by providing structure to the organizational events (Pentland, 1999). Sonenshein (2010) noted that narrative amended perceptions of organizational change initiatives by placing people on an equal footing. Specifically, they utilized the first person narrative (i.e. inclusive terminology) during managerial interviews when describing the importance of the change initiative. In a related piece of research to the current work, Author (2014) found that priming individuals with inclusive versus exclusive terminology increased the positive perceptions of job satisfaction. These findings illustrate an importance on the system of terminology utilized by organizational members, especially during change initiatives such as the cessation of the employment relationship (i.e. termination or downsizing). Based on this logic, it is hypothesized:

Hypothesis 1: Those individuals in the Inclusive Narrative condition will have significantly more positive perceptions of the termination interview than those individuals in the Exclusive Narrative condition.

Study1 - Methodology

Participants

Upper level undergraduate business students (N=60) participated in exchange for extra credit in which 29 were male and 31 were female with a mean age of 22.11 years. 32 participants (53.3%) were currently employed, 60 had currently or previously held a job (100.0%), and 9 (15.0%) had previous managerial experience.

Materials

The current study utilized several multi-item scales from Wood and Karau (2008) to measure the following reactions to the termination interview. Specifically we measured the following employee perceptions and reactions : a) Felt Anger (α = .79), b) Lack of Respect (α = .75), c) Willingness to take action (α = .94), d) Speak out (α = .72), e) Boss/Empathy (α = .77), f) Treated (α = .75), g) Respect (α = .80), and h) Willingness to request information (α = .71). Each of the scales are measured on a 9-point Likert type scale with higher scores representing more negative evaluations/perceptions of the termination interview.

Procedure

Participants were recruited in their classroom. At the beginning of the class period the study was passed out and the directions were explained. The first page of the materials asked respondents to sign a consent form to proceed with the study. The second page asked pertinent demographic information (see Appendix B) from the respondents. The third and fourth tasks included the termination scenario and Karau and Wood (2008) perceptions of terminations scale.

Study 1 - Results

Reactions to the Termination Interview

The overall MANOVA showed a number of significant effects, therefore we followed up with a series of univariate ANOVAS on each measure.

Felt Anger. There was a significant main effect for managerial narrative, $F (1, 60) = 23.166$, $p<.000$. Participants felt higher levels of anger in the exclusive condition (M = 5.67) than those in the inclusive condition (M = 4.13).

Lack of Respect. There was a significant main effect for managerial narrative, $F (1, 60) = 43.172$, $p<.000$. Participants felt higher levels of anger in the exclusive condition (M = 4.91) than those in the inclusive condition (M = 3.21).

Willingness to Take Action. There was a significant main effect for managerial narrative, $F (1, 60) = 63.096$, $p<.000$. Participants felt higher levels of anger in the exclusive condition (M = 3.97) than those in the inclusive condition (M = 1.91).

Willingness to Speak Out against the Company. There was a significant main effect for managerial narrative, $F(1, 60) = 50.298$, $p<.000$. Participants felt higher levels of anger in the exclusive condition ($M = 5.62$) than those in the inclusive condition ($M = 3.78$).

Felt your Boss had Empathy for you. There was a significant main effect for managerial narrative, $F(1, 60) = 23.580$, $p<.000$. Participants felt higher levels of anger in the exclusive condition ($M = 5.89$) than those in the inclusive condition ($M = 4.63$).

Felt they were Treated Fairly. There was a significant main effect for managerial narrative, $F(1, 60) = 22.510$, $p<.000$. Participants felt higher levels of anger in the exclusive condition ($M = 3.83$) than those in the inclusive condition ($M = 2.60$).

Felt they were treated with Respect. There was no significant main effect for managerial narrative, $F(1, 60) = 2.451$, $p<.ns$. Participants felt higher levels of anger in the exclusive condition ($M = 2.57$) than those in the inclusive condition ($M = 2.16$).

Willingness to Request Information. There was a significant main effect for managerial narrative, $F(1, 60) = 19.845$, $p<.02$. Participants felt higher levels of anger in the exclusive condition ($M = 6.80$) than those in the inclusive condition ($M = 5.65$).

Brief Discussion

The current study sought to assess the ability of managerial narrative to impact perceptions of termination interviews. In other words, can the words that management uses cause individuals to make different judgments of the fairness of an organizational event such as being terminated. The current findings suggest that the narrative utilized by management is capable of altering one's perception of a myriad of different perceptions/evaluations of terminations. Specifically, the utilization of inclusive terminology produced significantly more positive (less negative) perceptions of an individual's satisfaction level with the termination interview. Because termination interviews are only one way an individual may be terminated (i.e. they are terminated individually) a second study was designed to assess the influence on managerial narrative to impact a second perspective (i.e. being terminated in a collective) of downsizing. Based on the logic posited in the first study, it is assumed that perceptions of downsizing will be more positive (less negative) when utilizing inclusive as opposed to exclusive terminology.

> **Hypothesis 2:** Those individuals in the Inclusive Narrative Condition will have significantly more positive perceptions of downsizing than those individuals in the Exclusive Narrative condition.

Study 2 - Methodology

Participants

Upper level undergraduate business students (N=50) participated in exchange for extra credit in which 30 were male, 20 were female. . The mean age was 23.49 years of age. 37 participants (74.0%) were currently employed, 49 had currently or previously held a job (98.0%), and 19 (38.0%) had previous managerial experience.

Materials

The current study utilized a 20 item scale from Authors (2015) that measures general downsizing attitudes ($\alpha = .891$). The choice of this scale was appropriate because the purpose of the current study was to merely assess whether or not managerial narrative impacted perceptions of downsizing which the current scale measures. The scale was scored so that higher scores represent more positive perceptions of downsizing.

Procedure

Participants were recruited in their classroom. At the beginning of the class period the study was passed out and the directions were explained. The first page of the materials asked respondents to sign a consent form to proceed with the study. The second page asked pertinent demographic information from the respondents. The third and fourth tasks included the downsizing scenario and Authors (2015) downsizing attitudes scale.

Study 2 - Results

Manipulation

To test Hypothesis 1, the means of the scale was analyzed via a between-subjects analysis of variance (ANOVA). There was a significant main effect, $F (1, 50) = 5.157$, $p<. 03$ $\acute{\eta}^2 = .097$ such that those individuals in the Inclusive condition (M = 3.37) had significantly less positive perceptions of organizational downsizing than those in the Exclusive condition (M = 3.70; p <.03).

Brief Discussion

The current study was designed to measure if there were similar influences of managerial narrative on downsizing perspectives. Specifically, as in Study 1, did inclusive terminology lead to significantly more positive (less negative) perceptions of downsizing. Counter to predictions, and previous research in a similar area, exclusive terminology created more positive (less negative), as opposed to less positive (more negative), views of downsizing. This finding is interesting because it suggests a distinct and different perception of how one should be "talked to" during the cessation of the employment relationship when being terminated individually versus in a collective.

Discussion

The current research conducted a 2 study package in order to assess whether or not the nature of managerial narrative could influence perceptions of one's satisfaction levels following the cessation of the employee-employment relationship. As expected, Study 1 found that inclusive terminology created significantly higher levels of satisfaction than using exclusive terminology when conducting termination interviews. Study 2 found a significant influence on satisfaction levels following downsizing but in the opposite direction predicted. In other words, exclusive, not inclusive, terminology created higher levels of satisfaction.

The current findings have several important implications. For managers, wording matters. The nature or decision to focus on certain types of wording (inclusive versus exclusive) can alter an individual's evaluation of important organizational change events such as the cessation of the employment relationship. Furthermore, this is an effective means for increasing said levels of satisfaction because words are cheap. It does not cost the organization any money to use them. The organizational members simply need to be mindful of the wording they choose to use. A second implication is for theory. Managerial narrative needs to draw more attention from organizational scholars as it appears to be able to influence perceptions of important organizational change events. Future research should seek to answer the following questions: "what other terminology impacts one's perceptions?", "what other constructs can be impacted?", "does it matter who speaks the words?", and "what other contextual factors should research consider?".

Taking all of these things into account, the main contribution of the current research is the proposal of a new model of understanding perceptual outcomes that directly impact organizations. The current findings suggest a potential disconnect or disassociation individuals draw when evaluating the two situations. This disassociation or disconnect is what the current work terms the "psychological disconnect". A psychological disconnect is proposed as a psychological or cognitive evaluation process where an individual derives or focuses on different contextual variables and thus alters or flips the expected evaluation or outcome. In other words, it is likely that individuals terminated in a large group, such as a downsizing initiative, likely see this as being more of a business decision and less to do with themselves or their quality of work. Put differently, they may see this organizational outcome as being outside of one's control. On the other hand, an individual being terminated (as done in Study 1) by individually is likely to draw the conclusion that the situation is either personal or solely focused on one's ability to perform. Thus the current research posits a separate evaluation outcome (a more positive evaluation of downsizing while a more negative association of terminations event though the same terminology is being used) based on one's ability to psychologically distance themselves from the decision of the organization, a psychological disconnect. This psychological disconnect is likely to influence many other evaluations an individual makes on a daily basis. The extent to which an individual feels more harshly about a friend or family one being disadvantaged at work, as opposed to a complete stranger, suggests a shortening of the psychological disconnect. In other words, they are likely to feel more intense emotions because they are psychologically more connected with the individual being impacted (a friend or family member) as compared to the stranger. In fact, Author (2015) found that individuals can be supraliminally primed to alter their interpersonal distance (psychologically proximity to another). Specifically, individuals were primed by plotting points on a Cartesian plane where the distance between the two points plotted made a resulting line that was either significantly shorter than others or longer. The result of this was a decreased felt perception of justness or unjustness of an organizational initiative when evaluating the treatment of one's self versus others (especially when the other was an out-group member). Thus, the more similar an individual considers another individual to be to them, the more felt or more intense the perceptions of justness or unjustness are.

Other research in the organizational theory literature, which did not directly search for the proposed notion of a psychological disconnect, may glean some more supporting evidence of such a disconnect. For example, Porac, Thomas, and Baden-Fuller (1989) found that organizations have demonstrably different perceptions of who they compete against based on their mental model or perception of who is most likely to impact them. This suggests that while some organizations may narrowly define their competitor list, others may more broadly define it, thus they will respond to more competitive actions since they feel they must compete against these other individuals. In the terminology of the proposed model, the extent in which an individual narrowly or broadly defines who they compete against is a reflection of the psychological disconnect that individual has with the competing company. Thus, some will be more psychologically disconnected (i.e. won't consider a company a threat thus not a competitor) while others will perceive a greater degree of psychological connection (i.e. will consider as company a threat and a direct competitor). And what is interesting about this connection is that psychological disconnection or connection may explain why a manager at one local store responds or feels a need to respond to more competitive actions whereas another manager at the same store more narrowly defines who they compete with and thus does not feel they need to respond to competitive actions from all of the companies the first manager did.

Conclusion

In conclusion, the current research found that managerial narrative directly impact perceptions of the cessation of the employment relationship. Specifically, inclusive terminology is able to more positive influence perceptions of termination interviews while exclusive terminology is able to more positively influence perceptions of downsizing. These counterintuitive findings provide the initial foundation for what the current work terms "psychological disconnect". More research needs to be conducted to assess the influence of a psychological (dis)connection on one's evaluations or perceptions important organizational initiatives.

References

Armstrong-Stassen, M. 2002. 'Designated Redundant but Escaping Lay-off: A Special Group of Lay-off Survivors', *Journal of Occupational & Organizational Psychology, 75*(1), 1-13.

Authors [Name removed to preserve Anonymity] (2015). General Downsizing Attitudes: Scale Development and Empirical Assessment. *Under Review*

Bayer, R. 2000. Termination With Dignity, *Business Horizons*, October-October.

Bennett, N., Martin, C. L., Bies, R. J., & Brockner, J. (1995). Coping with a layoff: A longitudinal study of victims. *Journal of Management, 21*, 1025-1040.

Bies, R. J., Martin, C. L., & Brockner, J. (1993). Just laid off, but still a "good citizen". Only if the process is fair. *Employee Responsibilities and Rights Journal*, 6, 227-238.

Boatright, J. 2003. Ethics and the Conduct of Business (Prentice Hall, NJ).

Brockner, J. 1988. 'The Effects of Work Layoffs on Survivors: Research, Theory, and Practice', *Research in Organizational Behavior, 10*, 213-255.

Brockner, J. 1994. 'Perceived Fairness and Survivors' Reactions to Layoffs, or How Downsizing Organizations Can Do Well By Doing Good', *Social Justice Research, 7*, 345-363.

Brockner, J. (2002). Making sense of procedural fairness: How high procedural fairness can reduce or heighten the influence of outcome favorability. *Academy of Management Review, 27*, 58-76.

Brockner, J. (2006). Why it's so hard to be fair. *Harvard Business Review, 84*, 122-129.

Brockner, J., Davy, J., & Carter, C. 1985. 'Layoffs, Self-Esteem, and Survivor Guilt: Motivational, Affective, and Attitudinal Consequences', *Organizational Behavior and Human Decision Process, 36*, 229-244.

Brockner, J., Grover, S., O'Malley, M. N., Reed, T., & Glynn, A. 1993. 'Threat of Future Layoffs, Self-Esteem and Survivors' Reactions: Evidence From the Laboratory and the Field', *Long Range Planning, 26*, 152-152.

Brockner, J., Grover, S., Reed, T., Dewitt, R., & O'Malley, M. 1987. 'Survivors' reactions to layoffs: We get by with a little help for our friends', *Administrative Science Quarterly, 32*, 526-542.

Bruton, G. D., & Keels, J. K. (1996). Downsizing the firm: Answering the strategic questions. *Academy of Management Executive, 10*, 38-45.

Cascio, W. F. (1993). Downsizing: What do we know? What have we learned? *Academy of Management Executive, 7*, 95-104.

Cascio, W. F. (1998). Learning from outcomes: Financial experiences of 311 firms that have downsized. In M. K. Gowing, J. D. Kraft & J. C. Quick (Eds.), The New Organizational Reality: Downsizing, Restructuring, and Revitalization. (pp. 55-70). Washington, D.C.: American Psychological Association.

Cascio, W. F., Young, C. E., & Morris, J. K. (1997). Financial consequences of employment-change decisions in major U.S. corporations. *Academy of Management Journal, 40*, 1175-1189.

Clair, J. A., Dufresne, R., Jackson, N., & Ladge, J. (2006). Being the bearer of bad news: Challenges facing downsizing agents in organizations. *Organizational Dynamics, 35*, 131-144.

Cobb, A. T., Wooten, K. C., & Folger, R. (1995). Justice in the making: Toward understanding the theory and practice of justice in organizational change and development. In W. A. P. R. W. Woodman (Ed.), Research in organizational change and development (pp. 243-295). Greenwich, CT: JAI Press.

Cobb, S., and Kasl, S. 1977. 'Termination: The Consequences of Job Loss', Report # 76-1261, Washington D.C., *National Institute for Occupational Safety and Health.*

De Meuse, K. P., Vanderheiden, P. A., & Bergmann, T. J. (1994). Announced layoffs: Their effect on corporate financial performance. *Human Resource Management, 33*, 509-530.

Fiedler, F. E. 1964. 'A Contingency Model of Leadership Effectiveness', In L. Berkowitz (ed.), Advances in Experimental Social Psychology, Vol. 1, 149-190. New York: Academic Press.

Fisher, S. R., & White, M. A. (2000). Downsizing in a learning organization: Are there hidden costs? *Academy of Management Review, 25*, 244-251.

Folger, R., & Skarlicki, D. P. (1998). When tough times make tough bosses: Managerial distancing as a function of layoff blame. *Academy of Management Journal, 41*, 79-87.

Gilland, S. and Schepers, D. 2003. 'Why We Do the Things We Do: A Discussion and Analysis of Determinants of Just Treatment in Layoff Implementation Decisions', *Human Resource Management Review, 13*(1), 59-84.

Goleman, D. 1998. 'What Makes a Leader?', *Harvard Business Review*, 82(1), 82-91.

Greenberg, J. 1990. 'Organizational Justice: Yesterday, Today, and Tomorrow', *Journal of Management, 16*, 249-372.

Grunberg, L., Moore, S., & Greenberg, E. S. (2006). Managers' reactions to implementing layoffs: Relationship to health problems and withdrawal behaviors. *Human Resource Management, 45*, 159-178.

Hepworth, S. 1980. 'Moderating Factors of the Psychological Impact of Unemployment', *Journal of Occupational Psychology, 53*, 139-146.

Jesseph, S. 1989. 'Employee Termination: Some Dos and Don'ts', *Personnel, 66*, 36-38.

Kates, N., Greiff, B. and Hagen, D. 1990. 'The Psychological Impact of Job Loss', American Psychiatric Press.

Kinicki, A. J., Prussia, G. E., & McKee-Ryan, F. M. (2000). A panel study of coping with involuntary job loss. *Academy of Management Journal, 43*, 90-100.

Leana, C. R., & Feldman, D. C. 1988. 'Individual Responses to Job Loss: Perceptions, Reactions, and Coping Behaviors', *Journal of Management, 14*, 375-389.

Leana, C. R., & Feldman, D. C. 1990. 'Individual Responses to Job Loss: Empirical Findings From Two Field Studies', *Human Relations, 43*, 1155-1181.

Leana, C. R., & Feldman, D. C. (1992). Coping with Job Loss. New York: Lexington Books.

Miller, R. 2001. 'The Four Horsemen of Downsizing and the Tower of Babel', *Journal of Business Ethics, 29*, 147-151.

Nigro, L. and Waugh, W. 1996. 'Violence in the American Workplace: Challenges to the Public Employer', *Public Administration Review*, *56*, 326-332.

Noronha, E., & D'Cruz, P. (2005). Achieving downsizing: Managerial perspectives. *Global Business Review, 6*, 77-94.

Noronha, E., & D'Cruz, P. (2006). A necessary evil: The experiences of managers implementing downsizing programmes. *The Qualitative Report, 11*, 88-112.

O'Neill, H. M., & Lenn, D. J. 1995. 'Voices of Survivors: Words that Downsizing CEOs Should Hear', *Academy of Management Executive, 9*, 25-34.

Porac, J.F., Thomas, H., & Baden-Fuller, C. (1989). Competitive groups as cognitive communities: The case of Scottish knitwear manufacturers. *Journal of Management Studies*, 26, 397-416.

Pugh, S. D., Skarlicki, D. P., & Passell, B. S. 2003. 'After the Fall: Layoff Victims' Trust and Cynicism in Re-employment', *Journal of Occupational and Organizational Psychology, 76*, 201-212.

Quinley, K. 2003. 'Ten Ways to Prevent Employment Practices Claims After Layoffs', *Fair Employment Practices Guidelines*, 3/1/2003 Issue 571, 1-2.

Scher, S.J., & Heise, D.R. 1993. 'Affect and the Perception of Injustice', *Advances in Group Process, 10*, 223-252.

Schwieger, D. and Ivancevich, J. 1987. 'Executive Actions for Managing Human Resources Before and After Acquisitions', *Academy of Management Executive, 1*, 127-137.

Segal, J.A. 2009. '10 Things Not to Say When Firing an Employee', *BusinessWeek*, 11/10/2009

Shah, P. P. 2000. 'Network Destruction: The Structural Implications of Downsizing', *Academy of Management Journal, 43*(1), 101-112.

Sidebotham, E. 2005. 'How to Use Documentation to Decrease the Likelihood of Litigation', *The Psychologist – Manager Journal, 8*,131-140.

Vallero, D. A., & Vesilind, P. A. 2006. 'Preventing Disputes with Empathy', *Journal of Professional Issues in Engineering Education & Practice, 132*, 272-278.

Walker, Sean (2014). The Nonconscious Influence of Organizational Perceptions through Interpersonal Distance: An Experimental Study of Self versus Others. *Journal of Marketing Perspectives, 1*, 72-89.

Walker, Sean (2015). The Nonconscious Influence of Managerial Narrative on Perceptions of Job Satisfaction. *Journal of Marketing Perspectives, 1*, 6-27.

Wayhan, V. B., & Werner, S. (2000). The impact of workforce reductions on financial performance: A longitudinal perspective. *Journal of Management, 26*, 341-363.

Wood, M.S., & Karau, S.J. 2008. 'Preserving Employee Dignity During the Termination Interview: An empirical examination', *Journal of Business Ethics, 86*, 519-534

Woodward, J. 1958. '*Management and Technology*', London, H.M.S.O.

Zinn, L. 1988. 'Handing Out Pink Slips Gracefully', *Business Week*, 6/20/88 Issue 3057, 168-169

About the Author

Dr. Sean Walker earned his PhD from Southern Illinois University Carbondale in 2012 and an MBA from Southern Illinois University Carbondale in 2007. Currently he is an assistant professor of behavioral management at The University of Tennessee at Martin. He has authored numerous articles in organizational behavior and priming.

Appendix A - Brayfield & Rothe Index

Some jobs are more interesting and satisfying than others. We want to know how people feel about a hypothetical job. This blank contains eighteen statements about different aspects of a job. You are to write the number that best describes how you feel about your hypothetical job after reading the scenario. There are no right or wrong answers. We would like your honest opinion on each one of the statements.

1	2	3	4	5
Strongly Disagree	Disagree	Undecided	Agree	Strongly Agree

_____1. My job is like a hobby to me

_____2. My job is usually interesting enough to keep me from getting bored

_____3, It seems that my friends are more interested in their jobs.

_____4. I consider my job rather unpleasant

_____5. I enjoy my work more than my leisure time

_____6. I am often bored with my job

_____7. I feel fairly well satisfied with my present job.

_____8. Most of the time I have to force myself to go to work

_____9. I am satisfied with my job for the time being

_____10. I feel that my job is no more interesting than others I could get.

_____11. I definitely dislike my work

_____12. I feel that I am happier in my work than most other people

_____13. Most days I am enthusiastic about my work

_____14. Each day of work seems like it will never end

_____15. I like my job better than the average worker does

_____16. My job is pretty uninteresting

_____17. I find real enjoyment in my work

_____18. I am disappointed that I ever took this job

Appendix B – Demographic Data

1. Are you presently employed?
_____ Yes; Full-time
_____ Yes; Part-time
_____ No

2. How many years of work experience do you have? _____

3. How many years of managerial experience do you have? _____

4. Age _____

5. Gender
_____ Male
_____ Female

6. Country of birth
_____ United States
_____ Other

7. Ethnicity
_____ Caucasian (white)
_____ African American
_____ Asian American
_____ Hispanic
_____ Other, please specify: _____

The Cultural Myopia and Cultural Blindness in Overseas Management

S.M. Jameel Hasan
Eastern Washington University

ABSTRACT

Myopia means a lack of clear-sightedness and foresightedness, a restricted and blurred view of things. A myopic person, then, is someone who is shortsighted, lacking in perspicacity, with diminished capacity to see and evaluate the facts and the contexts as they actually are. In today's global business environment, as cross-cultural relations become even more embedded within the American infrastructure, there is an increasing need to understand and connect with a highly heterogeneous network by beginning to adopt a global "habit of mind" and global "habit of heart."

According to the many comprehensive systematic research studies of multicultural influences on the workplace, have found that culture is more frequently source of conflict than of synergy, largely due to cultural myopia and cultural blindness (Catino, October, 2014 ; Hofstede, 2010 –Appendix contains one page summary of Hofstede's research into national cultures and Culture's consequences) .

Global mindset is the ability to accept and work with cultural diversity, reflected in research that tries to map the skill or competence associated with management diversity. Cultural self-awareness and openness to and understanding of other cultures are the core elements of the psychological or, as some scholars prefer to label it, the cultural perspective on global mindsets (Schmidt and Cohen, 2013

(Levy et al. 2007,"Cosmopolitism" has been proposed as an underlying dimension of the psychological /cultural perspective. The second perspective— The Strategic Perspective—on global mindset is beyond the scope of this paper, that expects the individuals to balance competing priorities that do emerge in international management processes, rather than to advocate one dimension at the expense of others. This paper is totally concerned with the cultural perspective of the state of mind (Evans, Pucik, and Bjo"rkman, 2011; Meyers, 2014).

The paper will provide:

1)Many interesting, humorous, and illuminating examples and short cases overseas managers face and realize how vital it is to understand how cultural differences affect trust, team work, understanding, conflict resolution and cooperation, and the business entities --while working with people from other countries (Ricks,1979,2006; Meyers,2014).

2) Research-based conceptual models and the rules deriving from them—if internalized without false assumptions and with substantial amount of patience and humility to suspend judgment about numerous complex human entanglements at work and moving around in the country's different communities, especially dealing with the local governmental officials (Lee, 1966; Meyers.2014).

The paper furnishes many illustrative behavioral examples of cross-cultural myopia, blindness, and ugly and hurtful cultural clumsiness that the countries every year lose enormous amounts of money and reputational capital to their rival countries that are culturally and cross-culturally correct and wise, nimble, cultural savvy to leverage diversity, sensitive, and demonstrating empathy-centered attitudes and behaviors with humility and true respect—and they are successful in creative cultural adaptation of an individual dimension in overseas business situations that demand a certain level of knowledge of traits of the American culture and a similar level of understanding of the foreign culture(Lee,1966; Meyers,2014).

Stereotyping people from diverse cultures on just one or two dimensions can lead to erroneous assumptions. It is not at all surprising that even cosmopolitan managers—with decades of cross-cultural continuous contacts, interactions and connections—often have faulty expectations. Language fluency does not equate cultural fluency—each culture has different origins, dress, language of time, language of space, language of objects, language of gifts, language of corruption and influence peddling, social behavior patterns, and cross-cultural business customs--like how to address your host, bowing and hand-shaking, lateness for appointment, postponement in getting down to business, to belch or not belch after dinner at your host's home, eye-contact, proper way of presenting your Business Card in different countries, cross-cultural jokes and metaphors, respect for age, direct, clear, and brief talk as compared to quite vague but polite conversation about general topics or politics or host's family; cultural boundaries of formality and informality, size of the office and quality of office furnishings as an indicator of status, and numerous shades, meaning of meaning and manifestations of cross-cultural non-verbal behaviors in different cultural situations, and the use of alcohol and smoking cigarettes in the host's expensive and clean home and or in office or on the company premises.

In the new era of global and cross-cultural connectedness one must be perceptive, attentive, and agile to gain insight and have hopefully correct perception of social/business/government situations and the quick emergence of the novel and sometime highly embarrassing cross-cultural human encounters and incidents (Adekola and Sergi, 2007).

Introduction

Human factor is pivotal in the successful operations of the US domestic and global business operations. In the second decade of 21st century it is imperative US managers learn how to work more effectively with people from other countries and their sub-cultures. The challenge of *navigating cultural minefields* across the world requires real cross-cultural sensitivity and empathy at home and abroad in the real sense of managerial mantra: Be Truly Global In Terms Of: "Global Habit of Mind " and "Global Habit of Heart." (Lawler III and Boudreau, 2012).

Toward a Flat World?

Thomas Friedman's influential work *The World is Flat* (2005) suggests the "flat world" has produced a more level competitive playing field for individuals, groups, and companies from all parts of shrinking world. While the process of globalization was previously driven mostly by countries and then by corporations striving to expand their influence and integrate their activities is driven more by the ability of individuals, groups, and firms to collaborate and compete internationally using the tools of the increasingly *virtual world*—personal computers, smart phones, and work-flow software. Development in communications and transportation led to changes in internationalization in the past.

As the digital revolution becomes accessible all across the globe, this is happening all over again today. In today's economy, international HRM is increasingly global challenge for multinationals from all parts of the world. Human resource practices are more sensitive to local context than finance, marketing, and or manufacturing practices, because HRM deals with people, and people differ across the world:

"Every man is in certain respects (a) like all other men, (b) like some other men, (c) like no other man.(Kneller, 1971). The author of this paper believes in "essential unity of mankind"— *with a healthy respect for diversity in terms of feelings and senses, as opposed to intellect alone*.(Adler, 1939; Hutchins, 1953).

Ultimately, we are in a universe of people, by the people, and for the people. Should we must ignore cross-cultural perspectives, then we will do so at our own peril! The butterfly effect is of particular relevance. It just goes on to establish that while a product can be designed, marketed and sold with the best of brains behind it, it is finally a unique rapport with the target audience, riding on cultural understanding that will create the impact. If you dig very deeply into any problem, you will get 'people'.(IBM's William J. Wilson, 1966).

In the final analysis, people are creators and solvers of virtually any type of cross-cultural/global HRM problems (IBM's William J. Wilson, 1966).

Assumptions and Notions Underlying This Paper

1. Ethnocentric attitudes coupled with lack of ability to translate cultural empathy on the part of many overseas managers cause many problems concerning cross-cultural/global business relations.(Lee, 1966).

2. The global business firms face is that people are usually raised, trained and educated, and indoctrinated and oriented in one culture—where as global business management scenarios of the early decades of the 21st century and beyond require effective cross-cultural communication, supervision, creative adaptation, and coordination (Drucker, 1999).

3. It is very, very difficult for any person to *"get inside"* a culture that is not his own—despite the fact that one has spent, many, many years in an alien culture (Hall, 1960).

4."Be an *effective foreigner*" (Adler, 1991) rather than "*Do as the Romans do* "(Arning, 1964; Fagiano, 1990; Francis, 1991).

5. Diversity of management culture around the globe rather than corporate global village where a common culture of management unifies the practice of business around the world (Kanter, 1991).

6. Culture is bigger than countries. Mexican and Bolivians are more the same than they are different. The Spanish language and Catholicism, for example, are just the first links of a very strong bondage. Professor Kanter's survey results were reported in the *Harvard Business Review* that cultural affinity more than geographic proximity was a major determinant of manager's views around the globe—"*Cultural Allies,*" were classified into different groups, for example, "*Group 3*" included Austria, Belgium, Finland, France, Germany, the Netherlands, and Sweden; and the survey classified Japan, South Korea, India, and Hungary as "*Cultural Islands*". (Kanter, Harvard Business Review Survey, 991).

7. The diversity and interplay of cultural variables among home country, host country, and corporate personality *("culture")* create serious conflicts and crashes between the firm and the host nation—and the challenge of this conflict must be managed/accommodated. (Schneider, 1988; Taoka and Beeman,1991;Grosse and Kujawa,1988).

Truly Global World Order and the Great Human Achievement of Technology

The former Secretary of State Henry Kissinger (2014, page 350 and page 360) in his insightful book, *World Order,* made the geopolitical prognostication that wisdom and foresight will be needed to avoid the hazards and ensure that the technological era fulfills its vast promise. It needs to deepen its preoccupation with the immediate through a better understanding of history and geography._ The inventors of the devices that have so revolutionized the collection and sharing of information can make an equal if *not greater contribution by devising means to deepen its conceptual foundation* (Kissinger, 2014).

The author is delighted with Dr. Kissinger's final precept for applauding the humanistic and moral judgment dimensions in these words:

"On the way to the first truly global world order, the great human achievements of technology must be fused with enhanced powers of humane, transcendent, and moral judgment." (Kissinger,2014, Page 360, last paragraph).

Cultural Perspectives on the State of Human Mind

The scope of cross-cultural communication involves the whole complex of human life with a myriad of individual variation within and between significantly diverse and dynamic cultural systems. As such, by necessity the gist and focus of the cross-cultural examples/cases is basically on the dominant, broad, central viewpoint/interpretation based on research, observations as a cultured and cross-cultured university professor of several decades standing, and impressions and perspectives of culturally savvy and exceptionally well-traveled practitioners of cross-cultural communications around the globe. For the convenience of readers, the following informative, incisive examples are presented—the sequence of examples is not classified according to topics, or geography, or any other important criteria, except the author's discretion as a senior professor of Multinational People Management:

- Culture clash as Chinese chief seeks to *"Pimp my Volvo"*. A culture clash between Volvo's European management and Zhejiang Geely Holding Group Co (GEELY.UL), the *Chinese brand's owner-- Li Shufu since 2010--* may have broader implications for *corporate China.*

If Geely prevails in refocusing Volvo on China's premium market with a luxury brand pandering to a Chinese taste for excess—V12 or V8 engines-- and 'bling'— luxury sedans like BMW 7-series or Mercedes S-class; Volvos are 4-cylinder and 6-cylinder cars and showing off has never been part of the Volvo brand. Volvo European management says ostentatious Chinese consumers are not our target market.

"Mistresses love BMWs; Coal mine owners and property developers drive Mercedes. Those rich people like to show off." The Swedish Volvo management believes in safe, solid and understated way, 4 or 6 cylinder cars—*"Small is Beautiful."*

It is reported that Swedish Volvo management in China whispered: "Vulgar Volvo? Li Shufu wants to Pimp my Volvo". (Norihiko Shirouzu, *Yahoo Finance Exclusive*, October 10, 2013, page 1-6).

- A surprising finding of a cross-cultural study of 377 Chinese and Russian entrepreneurs that women entrepreneurs have larger social networks for advice and resources. But, men surprisingly have larger emotional networks, the complex associations that provide warmth, praise, and support—and men apparently profit more from these emotional attachments than women do (Harvard University Gazette Archives, February 8, 2007).

- Every transition economy –and cultural system—is different, and the lessons for Poland are not likely to be the same as Vietnam; for large countries like Russia with eight time zones, and China, regional differences are also enormously complex and super-multidimensional in its expressive depth and breadth. (Hasan,2007,2010).

- *The cultural meaning of color* cannot be ignored, For example, *Pepsodent* reportedly tried to sell in regions of Southeast Asia through a promotion their toothpaste helped enhance white teeth. Some people in this area chewed betel nuts in order to achieve the social prestige of darkly stained teeth—a highly ineffective promotion. The slogan says, *"wonder where yellow went"* was perceived by many in the area as a racial slur. (Ricks, 1979) To the Chinese, red is a lucky color; Thai would prefer yellow as a lucky color;

- The combination of black white, blue is suggestive of a funeral to the Chinese. The combination of red and white is regarded OK for happy and pleasant occasions. (Ricks, 1979, 2006).

- *"Okay"* (Fingers circle) is good and accepted in the US, except in Brazil, it is considered obscene; the same gesture is considered impolite in Russia and Greece, while in Japan, it means *"money"*, and in Southern France means *"zero or worthless"* (Axtell, 1990).

- *"Smile"* is one universal action, one signal, "one form of communication *that is used and understood by every culture and in every country, no matter how remote."*(Axtell,1990)

- An American supervisor expects the employee should look him in the eye. If the employee evades his direct glance the supervisor judges that employee is "shifty," and may be trying to hide something. In many Asian and Latin American countries, however, it is a long-established habit for a person never to look an elder or person in authority, in the eye. To do so is considered impertinent (Hall, 1955; 1960; Carol, 2011).

- In many Moslem countries, linking arms around the shoulders of your wife would in most cases embarrassment, since such physical contact should be confined to private quarters. Japanese grimace when a foreign business friend walks into a home without removing his shoes at the doorsill. In Pakistan, Saudi Arabia, Thailand, and in many Moslem countries, it is considered rude and insulting to display the sole of the foot (Hall, 1955 & 1960).

In almost all the Moslem countries one should not eat with his left hand. In the U.S. it is understood, when someone says, "let us go for a drink," that each person will pay for his drink. However, in Pakistan and many other countries such an invitation implies that the person who suggests will pay for both or more of the invitees' drinks (Axtell, 1990). Some Chinese cultures feel it is polite to take a portion of each food served. One US managers learned of this custom only after taking some visiting Chinese business men to U.S. type self-serving cafeteria. Each Chinese wound up with three trays of food and the US manager exceeded his [guest] hospitality expense account (Knotts,1989).

- A researcher verbalized the implicit assumptions of American spatial language: Private is better than public, higher is better than lower, near is better than far, and in is better than out. (Athos, 1968).To a Latin American, a distance of two feet seem to him approximately what five feet would to an American. To him, Americans seem distant and cold and unfriendly. To

Americans, he gives an impression of pushiness. As soon as the Latin American moves close enough for him to feel comfortable, the Americans feels uncomfortable and *"edges back"*(Hall, 1955;1960).

- In Japan, the top floor of a department store is reserved for the "bargain basement" and not for the offices of the top management. The French prefer to locate key managers in the center of activities, with their assistants located outward" on radii from this center" (Ball and McCulloch, 1990). As opposed to the American open-door policy, Germans regularly keep their office doors closed. The great Anthropologist Edward T. Hall indicates that the closed door does not mean that the manager behind it does not wish to have visitors but only that he deems open doors disorderly and sloppy(Hall, 1955;1960).

The Impact of Culture: Multiplicity of Contradictory Perspectives

- If one manages to extricate oneself from the culture that he is a product of, one would be extremely surprised to see how different the same world appears to be from another perspective. One should not dare offer beef to a Hindu or pork to a Muslim or an Orthodox Jew. Yet, some people in the Far East butcher dogs and consider their meat a delicacy. The same dogs are considered impure and not even touched by most Muslims; are badly treated and abused by people in many countries, kept as a strict necessity in most of Africa, respected as a unique form of life in India, and treated almost as members of the family by many Americans [In my Multinational People Management Seminar at least five students out of 30 students indicated in the seminar that they sleep either with their pet dogs or pet cats (Adekola and Sergi, 2007).

India holds about one-third of the world's livestock in their country. India assigns such strong social and economic values to its cattle that they are seen as religious symbols; Indian people have very high regard for cattle and treat them almost as individuals, and definitely as vital family-providers. Hence, there is a strong opposition to both killing and eating such animals (Adekola and Sergi, 2007, p. 201).

- A women visiting Brazil for business or vacation should know that people in Brazil are outgoing. Men tend to stare at and make comments about woman passing by. However, this is not considered rude and generally is ignored by the woman; a similar kind of incident happened to an American women professor who was a visiting professor in Eastern Europe she complained to the Country's Police with no effect on the police officer who simply laughed—case closed! (Adekola and Sergi, 2007,p.203)

- In Bolivia time is not as important as their significant feelings toward friendship are kindness, gentleness, and concern for another. American visitors better have some creative adaptive strategies to avoid unnecessary stress –"Time is money" (Adekola and Sergi, 2007, p. 204).

- In Quebec, Canada, the US sign of thumbs-down is also an offensive gesture and should be avoided. It is also offensive to burp in public, even if one excuses oneself. (Adekola and Sergi,2007, p.204)

- In France, slapping the open palm over a closed fist is vulgar. In addition, it is impolite to sit with your legs spread open or even with your legs crossed. One's feet are not to be placed on the table or chairs, and it is improper to speak with hands in the pockets or to chew gum in the public.(Adekola and Sergi,2007, p. 204)

- In Finland, the fashion standards are high and internationally recognized. Men must remove their hats when entering a building or elevator, or when speaking to another person. (Adekola and Sergi, 2007, p. 204).

- In Jamaica, Jamaicans take a flexible approach to time. If a manager were going to be assigned to a local to work, it would be good to inform the person of the following: A common good-natured answer to life's challenges is "No problem man," even if there is no solution at hand. In addition, events and meetings do not necessarily start on time. (Coon and Tyler, 1984).

- In Austin, Texas, visitors have to be prepared to do business over huevos rancheros (Adekola and Sergi, 2007, p.204).

- In Mexico, foods that include the main colors of the flag (green, white, and red) are popular on the Mexican table. Huevos rancheros, a classic Mexican dish, with avocados, sour cream and salsa, is a good example of this (Adekola and Sergi, 2007, p. 204).

- No two cultures share the same level of contexting. According to Dr. Edward T. Hall, the world authority on "Silent Language" and "Contexting", a correlation exists between face-saving and contexting. Cultures with high contexting are more concerned with face; that is, preserving prestige or outward dignity. Low context cultures are less concerned with face since words are more likely to be taken without underlying implied meanings.

As a result, high context cultures tend to favor a business communication approach based on indirection and politeness; low context cultures follow more of a confrontation strategy and use a direct plan approach to business communication. High context cultures view indirectness as honest and showing consideration while low context cultures view indirectness as dishonest and offensive. (Hall, 1976).

- In Japan and several other countries, many young business men take along an older man grey hair to lend his prestige to their cause. In the US, competence and performance on the given task counts, whether or not you have grey hairs (Hall, 1996, pp. 5-12). Many students in the US classes inquire about the market potential of hair-coloring products in these countries with growing older population.

- Red roses for a German lady mean "I'm in love with you!" White and yellow flowers are not good choices in many areas because they connote death (Reardon, 1984). In France,

112

yellow flowers suggest infidelity and should never be given—odd numbers of flowers are given, but not 12, and not an unlucky 13 (Business Week, December 6, 1976, p.91).

- Bargaining over price for a gift to give it your business friend is practically taboo in Britain or in the United States; it is not only permitted but expected in many parts of Europe, Africa, Latin America and the Far East (Hall, 1959; Klineberg, 1964, p. 135).

- In most of Latin America, especially in Spain, if a visitor expresses admiration of a vase or a picture, the host is likely to pick it up immediately and hand it to his guest with such words as "Take it...it is yours"; the latter may make the mistake this polite gesture for a genuine gift and got off with the object, much to the chagrin of the unwilling donor.

- On the other hand, in the Arab countries" do not admire the object openly, you may be the recipient of it, for example "what a handsome camel" (Klineberg, 1964:134-135; Axtell, 1990, p.80).

- Some of the most annoying difficulties for U.S. expatriates are based on local customs—in Switzerland, there is a law saying one cannot mow his lawn on weekend afternoons. (Brandt, March 1991).

- Never give gifts with the left hand in Saudi Arabia (the left hand is a toilet hand), never give a pig-skin purse or luggage or Scotch whiskey in the Arab world. The Japanese are great gift-givers and one cannot out gift them—they lose face if they are outdone. Give gifts with both hands in many Pacific Rim Countries including Japan where you never give an unwrapped gift or visit a Japanese home empty-handed. Japanese never give four(4) of anything or an item with four in the name because the word sounds like the one for death (Ball and McCulloch, 1990); also, do not give a potted plant when your Japanese friend is in a hospital, since you do not wish his illness to take "deeper roots" and get sicker. (BusinessWeek, Dec. 6, 1976, pp. 91-92).

- Your business card is the ultimate proof of your identity, rank, and profession. In Italy, even a bachelor's degree entitles to put a Dr. in front of your name (Axtell, 1990, p.8).

A Mexican individual with a B.A. degree in business administration entitles him to use the term "Licenciado" before his name. In some Southeast Asian countries a person will print his name, B.A., M.A.(Failed). In Japan, Southeast Asia, Africa, and the Middle East (except Israel) never present the card with your left hand. In Japan, present it with both hands, and make sure the type is facing the recipient and is right-side-up. (Axtell, 1990, page 8). "Do not leave home without your business card".

The Vocabulary of Time is Culturally Determined

A researcher talks about how many ways we, the Americans, talk about time. We have time, keep time, buy time, and save time; we mark it, spend it, sell it, and waste it; we kill time, pass time, give time, and take time, and every now and then, "make time" (Athos, 1968). The South Asians who say, "Come over and see me, see me anytime," means just that; many Iranians were puzzled by Americans usual message, "Well, I'll see you later." Iranians kept expecting to see American who never came to see them. In Japan, it is not unusual to have long periods of silence in the middle of negotiations between Japanese and American business men; although it may be nerve-racking, it is usually pays off handsomely if the Westerners can restrain themselves "to outwait the silence of his hosts. It may be thirty minutes, perhaps more" (Nation's Business, March, 1989). In Ethiopia, the more important a business matter, the more time is taken; whereas in the US, a delay is interpreted by the other party as a lack of interest. In Moslem countries the concept of tomorrow is in the hands of Allah [Insallah , God Willing; With the help of God] (Ball and McCulloch 1990; Skinner, 1968).

Punctuality is a virtue in the US, Holland, Switzerland, and in so many countries, but is relatively unimportant in Spain. The only time you must take punctuality seriously is when attending a bullfight (Adelkola and Sergi, 2007).

Conclusions

Applying the 4-step SRC Model for Punctuality—The Problem of Lateness for Appointments

The following are the four steps of the SRC Model:

Step 1: Define the business problem or goal in terms of the American cultural traits, habits, or norms.

Step 2: Define the business problem or goal in terms of the foreign cultural traits, habits or norms. Make No Value Judgments.

Step 3: Isolate the SRC influence in the problem and examine carefully to see how it complicates the problem.

Step 4: Redefine the problems without the SRC influence and solve for the optimal business goal situation—Creative Adaptation of the American and the Foreigner. The first step in this process is the isolation of the American self-reference criterion habit as a biasing influence. From this point, the knowledge required may be used in the solution of business problems in adaptation. Instead of measuring foreign cultures with an American-calibrated "culturometer," the American value system is set aside and a more internationally objective measurement system used in both cultures.

The SRC-free approach, which begins with two sets of cultural measures, permits a better bicultural fit to be discovered for the American business abroad. This SRC-free approach—Cultural Analysis—is further seen—in dealing with the problem of lateness for appointment-- to apply to individual manager adaptation abroad (Lee, 1966).

Step 1 of the SRC Model:

Are all Americans prompt? Is this promptness related to economic superiority? Americans have had the means to be on time for many generations. Good public transportation, many watches, smart phones, internet, computers, tablets, twitter, and many more communication facilities, and much practice in being punctual should be considered partly responsible. And Americans have the good fortune of being descended from time-conscious ancestors going back several centuries.

Step 2 of the SRC Model

In the foreign culture one can often readily see poorer transportation and communication facilities. In most cultures, where extreme poverty abound, there will be some kind of fatalism and get-through-the-day carryover from centuries of survival struggles which inhibit the habit of planning very far in the future. Moreover, it will be evident that the capabilities—education and skills-of those on whom a planned event depends are inferior.

Step 3 of the SRC Model

Our SRC can be seen to have prevented our noting carefully the basis on which On-Time Behavior depends. It has therefore produced expectancies on our part which are inconsistent with actual situational demands.

The above analysis thus far would indicate that under the circumstances a certain looseness in other culture's time system is both desirable and functional.

Step 4 of the SRC Model

How can the American adapt to this system? One solution would be for him to begin to plan on lateness. He can often arrange to be busy with other work until the foreigner arrives. He should also try to take comfort in the knowledge that his foreign visitor, when he does finally arrive, will be patient until the American substituted activity can be broken off. This is because the foreigner has developed a patience to fit the necessary looseness of his own culture's time system.

Conversely, if the appointment is at the foreigner's office, the American should take his briefcase, smart phone, laptop computer and other modern technological devices so he can be busy with other work until the foreigner can see him.

Moreover, you are true to your own American Culture: Time is money, wasting time induces guilt that motivates the American to get busy in other work and productively conserves time, practicing patience and suspending moral judgment-- that how dare this foreigner is trying to cool my heels in the waiting room—creates a cool, pleasant attitude and warmth in meeting and greeting this foreigner; Both win.

The Americans must also keep in mind that the foreigner operates on his own SRC and will probably assume that the American, like his own people, will be patient and understand the delay.

Cheers for the American and cheers for the foreigner engaged in becoming culturally sensitive and learning how to practice cultural empathy at home and abroad. It is imperative to feel the continuous nature of behavior in the new era of global connectedness (Toffler, 1990; Johnston, 1991) in order to gain awareness of and insight into social situations and accompanying circumstances.

Nicolas Berdyaev made the following brilliant observation:

> *"Science and scientific foresight give man power and security, but they can also devastate his consciousness and sever him from reality. Indeed, it might be said that science is based upon the alienation of man from reality, and of reality from man. The knower is outside reality, and the reality he knows is external to him. Everything becomes the object, i.e. foreign to man and opposed to him...the meaning of things is revealed not through their entering into man who is passive in relation to them, but through man's creative activity reaching out to meaning beyond an unmeaning world* (Berdyaev, 1960, pp.7-8).

Cultural myopia or cultural blindness is a significant factor in maintaining ethnocentric assumptions. Cultural diversity is a truism now, *and* recognition of this fact is paramount in cross-cultural business relations around the globe.

References

Adekola, A., & Sergi, B. (2007). *Global Business Management: A Cross-Cultural Perspective.*

Burlington, VT: Ashgate.

Adler, M. J. (1939). "The Crisis in Contemporary Education," *The Social Frontier,* 5, 141-14.

Arning, H. K. (1964). "Business Customs: From Malaya to Murmansk," *Management Review,* October 1964, 4-14.

Athos, A. G. & Coffey, R. E. (1968). *Behavior in Organization: A Multidimensional View,* Englewood, N.J.: Prentice-Hall..

Axtel, E. R. (ed.). (1990). *Do's and Taboos Around the World* (2nd .). New York: John Wiley & Sons.

Ball, D. A., & McCulloch, W. H. (1990). *International Business* (4th ed.). Homewood: Ill. Irwin/BPI.

Berdyaev, N. (1960). *The Destiny of Man.* New York: Harper.
"Cross-Cultural Customs and the Potted Plant and Japan." (1976). *Business Week. December 6:91-9*
Brandt,E. (1991). "Global HR," *Personnel Journal, March: 41.*

Carol, K. G. (2011). The Silent Language of Leaders: How Body Language Can Help-or-Hurt –How you Lead (1st ed.) San Francisco: Calif.: Jossey-Bass.

Catino, M. (2013).*Organizational Myopia : Problems of Rationality and Foresight in Organization,* New York: Cambridge University Press.

Coon, D.L. & Tyler, V. L.(1984). *Culturegrams.* Provo, UT: David M. Kennedy Center for International Studies, Brigham Young University.

Drucker, P. F. (1999). *The Futures That Have Already Happened.* New York: Harper.

Evans, P., Puick, V. & Bjo"Orkman (2011). *The Global Challenge: International Human Resource Management* (2nd ed.). NY: New York.

Fagiano, D. (1990). "Learning to Market As the Romans Do." *Management Review,* May: 4.

Friedman, T. (2005). " It's a flat world after all." *The New York Times Magazine,* April: 33.

Grosse, R., & Kujawa, D. (1988). *International Business.* Homewood , Ill: Irwin.

Hall, E. T. (1955). "The Anthropology of Manners." *Scientific American,* April: 85-86.

Hall, E. T. (1960). " Intercultural Communication: A Guide to Men of Action." *Human Organization,* Spring Issue: 8-9.

Hall, E. T. (1960). " The Silent Language in Overseas Business." *Harvard Business Review,* May-June: 87-96.

Hall, E. T. (1976). *Beyond Culture.* Garden City, New York: Doubleday

Harvard University Gazette Archives. (2007). February, 8.

Hofstede, G. (1980). *Culture's Consequences: International Differences in Work-Related Values.*Thousand Oaks, Calif.: SAGE Publications.

Hofstede, G. (1991). *Culture and Organization.* London: McGraw-Hill.

Hofstede, G. (1997). Cultures and Organaizations: Software of the Mind. London: McGraw-Hill

Hutchins, R. M. (1953). *The Conflict in Education.* N.Y: New York: Harpr.

Johnston, W. B. (1991). " Global Work Force 2000: The New World Labor Market, " *Harvard Business Review,* March-April: 115-127.

Kanter, R. M. (1991). "Transcending Business Boundaries : 12,000 World Managers View Change." *Harvard Business Review*, May-June: 152.

Kissinger, H. (2014). *World Order.* NY, New York: Penguin Press.
-14-
Klineberg, O (1964). *The Human Dimension in International Relation. NY,* New York: Holt, Rinehart and Winston.

117

Hutchins, R. M. (1953). *The Conflict in Education.* N.Y: New York: Harpr

Knotts, R. M. (1989). "Cross-Cultural Management: Transformations and Adaptation." *Business Horizons,* May-June: 29-33.

Lawler III, E. & Boudreau, J. W. (2012). *Effective Human Resource Management: A Global Analysis.* Palo Alto: California: Stanford Business Books.

Lee, J. A. (1966). "Cultural Analysis in Overseas Operations." *Harvard Business Review,* March-April: 107-114.

Meyer, E. (2014). "Navigating the Cultural Minefield." *Harvard Business Review,* May: 119-123.

"Blunders Abroad,"(1989). *Nation's Business.* March: 54-55.

Meyer, E. (2014). The Cultural Map: Breaking Through the Invisible Boundaries of Global Business. Public Affairs.

Reardon, K. (1984). International Business and Gift-Giving Customs.(2nd ed.). Janesville: Wisconsin: Parker Pen Company.

Schneider, S.C. (1988). "National vs. Corporate Culture: Implications for Human Resource Management," *Human Resource Management, 27(2): 231-246.*

Schmidt , E. & Cohen, Jared (2014). The New Digital Age: Transforming, Nations, Businesses, and Our Lives. Paperback edition, March: Vintage Reprint Edition.

Skinner, W. (1968). American Industry in Developing Economies. NY: New York: John Wiley & Sons

Tao, G.M., & Beeman, D.R. (1991). International Business. NY: New York: Harper Collins Publishers

Toffler, E. (1990). The Powershift. NY: New York: Bantam Books, Inc.

Wilson, W. J.[IBM Fame] (1966). "The Growth of a Company: A Psychological Case Study, " *Advanced Management Journal,* January: 43.

Appendix A - Summarizes Hofstede's research.

Research into National Cultures
Culture's Consequences, Geert Hofstede

5 Independent Dimensions –

- Inequality: more or less? Power Distance large vs. small
- The unfamiliar: fight or tolerate? Uncertainty Avoidance strong vs. weak
- Relation with in-group: Loose or tight? Individualism vs. Collectivism
- Emotional Gender roles: different or same? Masculinity vs. Femininity
- Need Gratification: later or now? Long vs Short term orientation

Small PD, Weak UA	**Large PD, Weak UA**
Nordic Countries	China
Anglo Countries, USA	India
Netherlands	
German Speaking Countries	Latin Countries
Hungary	Malta, Muslim Countries
Israel	Japan, Korea
	Eastern Europe
Small PD, Strong UA	**Large PD, Strong UA**

Collectivist, Feminine	**Collectivist, Masculine**
Thailand, Korea	China, Japan
Costa Rica, Chile	Mexico, Venezuela
Russia, Bulgaria	Arab World
Portugal Spain	Greece
Malta	Czechia, Hungary
France	Poland, Italy
Netherlands	German Speaking Countries
Nordic Countries	Angio Countries, USA
Individualist, Feminine	**Individualist, Masculine**

Implications of dimensions – Significant statistical relationships

- Examples (out of 400)
- Power Distance large: more perceived corruption
- Uncertainty Avoidance strong: stress on law and order
- Individualist, not collectivist: higher Human Rights rating
- Feminine, not masculine: higher welfare budgets
- Long-term, not short-term orientation: higher savings rates

NEW (Nurse Entrepreneurship Worldwide)

Kimberly DeSantis
Indiana University East

Timothy W. Scales
Indiana University East

ABSTRACT

The leadership characteristics of nurses enable them to provide health services globally. The nurses' clinical experience serves as the framework for the business and their knowledge and experience is transformable into a marketable service. Nurse consultants can assess an individual's needs, create a plan of care specific to that person, and implement a plan of care.

In this paper, the authors will share findings of practical issues and ways to create an economy within the healthcare community, the local community and even a global community utilizing nursing as entrepreneurship.

Keywords: Nursing, entrepreneurship, economics, community development, leadership

Introduction

While recent unemployment has spiked, signs of recession continue to be visible and governmental presence is more apparent in healthcare than any time in history creating an opening for nurse entrepreneurs. Yes, nurses creating jobs in a challenged economy.

Before leaving a job, an individual should feel comfortable with the uncertainty arising from that action and capable of taking on the associated risk. As an employee, you are paid for your time by your employer. But, a business owner, out of necessity, will spend a great deal of time in managerial and administrative work; including record keeping, hiring and training new employees. Entrepreneurship can be a very complex and ever changing environment when compared to that of a simple employee.

It's important to recognize expectations and sync them with your both short and long term goals. Individuals interested in pursuing an entrepreneurial role must make sure they have the personality and tenacity to succeed in this ever changing environment.

It's okay to start part-time.

The transformation of entrepreneurs to the role of human business heroes is an honorable and natural development for business leaders. The extent that entrepreneurship has captured the public attention is evident in the publication, *USA Today*. It surveyed young people, asking if they could devote one year to any occupation, what they would choose. For the women, 47% chose entrepreneur, more than tour guide or novelist. For the young men, 38% chose entrepreneur, even more than professional athlete. Increasingly, in many countries entrepreneurs are becoming heroic. A Gallup poll reported that more than 90% of Americans would approve if either a daughter or son attempting to start a small business (Dennis, 1997a).

The interest in entrepreneurship reflects what is happening in society as we become more aware of our need for independence. A few years ago, *Fortune* magazine estimated that the average young person entering the job market would have ten different jobs with five different organizations before retirement. Old industries decline and well-known corporate names disappear. Many young people recognize they must take responsibility for their own careers. Even if they expect to start with larger firms and hope to stay there for their entire career, circumstances and conditions evolve. Individuals who have developed entrepreneurial skills will be better prepared for a constantly changing world. These individuals may have more interesting and varied options in the future. It is clear that many of the careers offering the greatest rewards and excitement are in the entrepreneurial environment.

In 1969, only 274,000 new corporations were started; in 1998, that number had reached 761,000. Data suggest that, when all organizational entities, including part-time and home-based businesses are counted, the total number of start-ups seems to be on the order of 4.5 million per year, far higher than anyone had suspected (Dennis, 1997b).

High rates of change create opportunities and it is the entrepreneurial thinking that will have the opportunity to flourish in this reality. This time in history may become the decade of the entrepreneur if the opportunities are acted upon in a timely manner.

Public perception and acceptance of small business has never been better. A survey sponsored by NFIB indicated that 85% of the American public believes that small business is primarily a positive influence on the way things are going in this country. Seventy percent of the people think that owning a small business is one of the best ways to "get ahead". (Dennis, 1997a).
You can start your entrepreneurial venture part-time and keep your current employment and benefits. When the time is right, you will be ready to move to self-employment if it is for you. In the meantime, you will feel better about yourself, your frustrations will decrease, and you will have freed your creative spirit.

What products or services are you offering?

If you don't want to deal with improved products and services, you can market whatever specialty you want to help people. One must ask the question: am I ready to do the work necessary and commit to creating, marketing and delivering my selection of products and services to those people who want it?

Reasons for Becoming an Entrepreneur

One could say that an entrepreneur is a person who destroys the existing economic order by introducing new products and services. Creating new forms of organization or by exploiting new raw materials. This destruction can be done through forming a new business or by working within an existing business. Entrepreneurship is the process of creating something new with value through running a business by devoting the necessary time and effort, assuming the financial, psychic, and social risks, and receiving rewards of monetary and personal satisfaction and independence.

It may be time to explore becoming an entrepreneur if one is:

- Independent
- Confident
- Creative and Expressive
- Forward thinking
- Committed and Focused
- Self-Motivated, and Able to see things through

If you are beyond the Status Quo and it doesn't make sense how something is done a certain way, just because it's always been done that way. You don't like following the pack, so you are not seen as a 'team player', it may be time to become an entrepreneur. If you say, "I want to be my own boss" You're afraid of not pursuing your passion and idea. This fear is very common in our society because we've been conditioned to think that entrepreneurship is much more risky than getting a "steady job". In reality, both are risky in happiness, making a living and losing it all, it may be time to become an entrepreneur.

Opportunities Await Nursing Entrepreneurs

Definition of Nurse Entrepreneur

Nurse Entrepreneurship is a process which recognizes opportunity in a competitive health market to address issues of economics, service access, and the development of health services (McCline, Bhat, & Baj, 2000). A nurse entrepreneur develops, organizes, manages, and assumes the risks of a business. A nurse entrepreneur is a proprietor of a business that offers nursing services of a direct care, educational, research, administrative or consultative nature. The self-employed nurse is directly accountable to the client, to whom, or on behalf of whom, nursing services are provided (Gratton & Erickson, 2007). Nurse entrepreneurship provides an opportunity for experienced, well-qualified nurses to develop their expertise in clinical practice, research, education, and management, and continue to contribute their skills to the health sector. They are an important part of the health care system and provide the public with a greater degree of choice regarding health services.

Figures gathered by the International Council of Nurses estimated that 0.5-1% of registered nurses worldwide work in entrepreneurial roles (Wilson, Whitaker, & Whitford, 2012).

Possible Entrepreneurial Roles and Services could include:

Clinics-Nurse-run clinics help increase access to health care. Nurses can provide care, primary health care services, and traditional nursing services outside of normal business hours. These services can include minor injuries, emergencies, and chronic disease management. Preventive care services for diabetes, asthma, depression, and anxiety can also be provided by the clinics. Nurses are educated from a holistic perspective and can provide services such as complementary therapies, counseling, health promotion and prevention services.

Community based practices- Nurses work in the local community to provide multidisciplinary services for the elderly. These types of services allow elderly people to remain in their homes rather than be forced to enter residential care facilities (Wilson, Whitaker, & Whitford, 2012).

Education: Nurses can provide educational services such as communication, community skills, conflict management, occupational health and safety, and stress management. They can provide workshops and seminars on a variety of topics. Educational services also include writing educational materials. Nurses can provide education in single or group sessions. Fees for educational services can range from $41.00-$ 61.00 an hour.

Consultant: Consultant services focus on management matters and development of policies and services. These services can be provided to health organizations, educational facilities and legal companies. Legal nurse consultants use expertise as a health care provider to consult on medical-related legal cases.

Researcher: Nurses can provide research services to health facilities, educational programs, and health personnel. Services could include assisting with grant applications, research on aged care, forensic medicine, palliative care, and market research.

Conclusion

The future of entrepreneurship is exciting. Many students see themselves in an entrepreneurial role as they prepare themselves for a career following the many hours of college preparation. Alumni are often excited about programs related to entrepreneurship. The Coleman Foundation, the Price Foundation, the NFIB Foundation, and the Kauffman Foundation have all sponsored an impressive number of initiatives to encourage and support entrepreneurship research and education.

This is an important time to foster innovation among Registered Nurses in health care. Nurses play a critical role in the health care system. Nurses are more cost effective and increase access to care especially in areas where there is a lack of physicians. Entrepreneurship gives nurses the ability to seek roles that in which they are passionate. To engage in innovative behavior, nurses need management support, resources, a supportive work environment, and knowledge about innovation and the nurses' role. Nursing leadership is vital to the development of nursing practice that enables and supports the level of intensity necessary to the innovation process.

Nurses have an "incredible knowledge bank" that can be leveraged to achieve entrepreneurial success. It is time to evolve traditional nursing roles and become a Nurse Entrepreneur.

References

Dennis, W. J., Jr. (1997a). The public reviews small business. Washington, DC: NFIB Education Foundation.

Dennis, W. J., Jr. (1997b). More than you think: An inclusive estimate of business entries. *Journal of Business Venturing.* 12, p. 3.

Gratton, L., & Erickson, T. (2007). 8 ways to build collaborative teams. *Harvard Business Review, 85* (11). 100-109.

McCline, R.L., Bhat, S., & Baj, P. (2000). Opportunity recognition: An exploratory investigation of a component of the entrepreneurial process in the context of the health care industry. *Entrepreneurship: Theory and Practice, 25*(2), 81.

Wilson, A., Whitaker, N., & Whitford, D. (2012). Rising to the challenge of health care reform with entrepreneurial and intrapreneurial nursing initiatives. *Online Journals of Issues in Nursing ,* *17*(2). 1. doi: 10.3912/OJIN.Vol17No02 Man05.

About the Authors

Kimberly DeSantis, Ph.D., RN, has 15 years of teaching experience in RN-BSN, BSN, and MSN nursing programs at Indiana University East. She earned her undergraduate Bachelor of Science in Nursing and Master's of Science in Nursing Education at Wright State University in Dayton, Ohio. She completed her Ph.D in Adult Education at Capella University. Dr. DeSantis' area of expertise is in community nursing and service learning. She has served as a clinical course coordinator for many years and is responsible for mentoring adjunct clinical faculty. As an educator, Dr. DeSantis is constantly seeking opportunities to facilitate critical thinking, reflection, and empowerment through service learning clinical experiences.

Tim Scales earned a B.S. in Business at Indiana University East, a MBA from Anderson University and a Graduate Degree in Banking from the University of Wisconsin at Madison. He is also a graduate of the Disney Institute for Leadership Excellence. In addition to his degrees, Tim has a license in real estate and insurance. He serves as the director of the Center for Entrepreneurship and the Center for Economic Education at Indiana University East, and is a lecturer in the School of Business and Economics. As a School of Business Senior Faculty member, he meets with and mentors students as they develop their business skills. He has presented at various economic and entrepreneurship conferences nationally and internationally and was a guest instructor at St. Xavier University in India, the Community Chamber in Tunisia, Mexico City, Mexico and recently lectured in South Africa.

Tim Scales is an entrepreneur and the owner of A Fortune 500 Company. He is the host and executive producer of "In Your Business". "In Your Business" has spotlighted over 200 businesses on the local cable network, WCTV. He also provides the venue for high school and college students to interact with community leaders at monthly "Linens and Leaders" dinners. Education is a primary focus for Tim

~~Call for Papers~~

Academy of Business Research
Spring 2016 International Conference

New Orleans, LA

March 23-25, 2016
Renaissance Hotel, New Orleans

www.aobronline.com

Deadline

Abstract submissions for the Spring 2016 International Conference are due by February 6, 2016. All completed abstracts must be submitted via email to info@academyofbusinessresearch.com or through this online submission form. Abstracts must include all authors, institutional affiliation, and email information. Acceptance decisions will be made no later than February 13, 2016.